THE
TRICKY BIT

**A father and sons cycling adventure
through Kyrgyzstan, China and Pakistan**

PETER CHARLESWORTH

THE TRICKY BIT
A father and sons cycling adventure through
Kyrgyzstan, China and Pakistan

Published by Peter Charlesworth in 2024
www.openmatter.com

ISBN: 9781738475506

CONTENTS

Our route 5

Introduction 7

Crazy idea! 10

Tragedy in Tajikistan 17

Okay Dad let's get going 21

Made it to Xinjiang 26

The chase to Kashgar 30

On the run from the Chinese police 36

Highest paved border crossing in the world ... 54

Huge mountains and beautiful villages 78

Thank you Pakistan police 85

Winding roads through mountains and valleys ... 87

Welcome to Abbottabad 94

Tough ride to Islamabad 104

Lahore markets and mosques 108

Wagah border rejection. Thanks India! 114

Islamabad Indian embassy 117

Murree mountain resort 119

Struggle to New Delhi 124

About the author 129

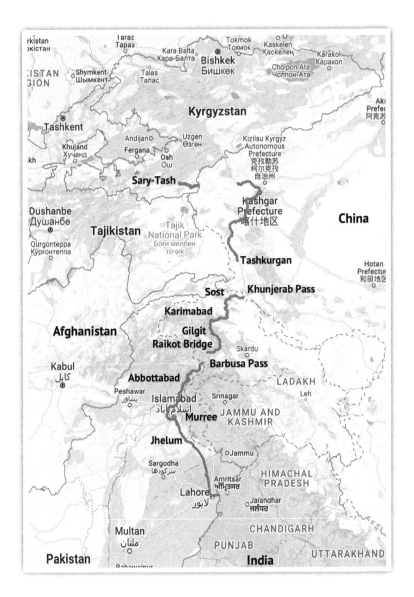

INTRODUCTION

Pedr grew up asking us to tell him 'real stories' at bedtime. He loved all sorts of stories, but real ones were his favourite. He insisted that we include all the details, and asked everybody in the family to recount every story they could remember. We were lucky as a family to have plenty of these, and were very happy to recount them for him. They were mostly from the many family holidays we had, climbing and exploring the mountainous areas of the world.

It really shouldn't have come as a surprise that, as soon as he had completed his studies, Pedr came home from university with his plan.

'Dad, Mum, I have something to say, best sit down.'

And so it unfolded that Pedr, having now obtained his master's degree in chemistry, was going to cycle around the world for the next couple of years.

So how did this extend to involve me? Well, it went like this:

'What route are you taking around the world, Pedr?' I instinctively asked. 'Which countries do you need to cycle through?'

Everything looked good until he reached the part about Asia. Here the options boiled down to cycling thousands of miles through the deserts of China and Mongolia, which didn't appeal to him at all; or, cycling through China's Xinjiang province – beginning in Kyrgyzstan, crossing into China, then through the city of Kashgar and following the Karakoram Highway over the highest border pass in the world, the Khunjerab Pass, through Pakistan, over the Karakoram and Himalayan mountains, and across the Wagah border to India.

The British consulate's advice could have been better, and I quote: 'The Foreign and Commonwealth Office (FCO) advise against all travel on the Karakoram Highway between Islamabad and Gilgit'. It went on to state how 'There is a high threat of terrorism, kidnap and sectarian violence throughout the country, including the cities of Islamabad, Rawalpindi, Lahore and Karachi'.

The Karakoram Highway (and most of those cities) were exactly Pedr's planned route, and he was adamant he was going to try and cycle it all.

Annwyl, my wife, answered with:

'Dad must come with you for protection. Two cyclists are safer than one, right?'

Before I was even able to assess the situation, the deal had been done. I was to somehow get two months off work, train to be an Olympian cyclist capable of scaling the Himalayas on a fully loaded twenty-three-year-old bike (the one I bought for £199 when Pedr was only one year of age), and then protect Pedr from terrorists and bandits along 1,700 miles of severe deserts, huge climbs and weather that ranged from forty-five degrees and eighty-five percent humidity to being snowbound in the high mountains. This was going to be the biggest challenge of my life.

Pedr set off from home on his bike on 20 January 2018, just as severe arctic weather (now remembered as the 'Beast from the East') hit Europe, while I set about adding panniers to my bike and trying to get some training rides through the gently rolling Chiltern hills of Buckinghamshire.

August came along way too quickly and I found myself with my bike in a box heading for Heathrow to fly to Bishkek in Kyrgyzstan to meet up with Pedr.

Eeeek! I thought. *What have I done?!*

This is a summary of our adventures over the eight weeks that followed.

CRAZY IDEA!

'That's a great idea, but you must be completely mad.'

That was one of the most positive comments from our friends. The others are unprintable.

This was a mammoth physical undertaking even for a fit twenty-three year old. My bones, by comparison, were twenty-three about thirty-two years ago.

My mum, being very adventurous herself, was extremely supportive of my plan to join Pedr. She would of course have preferred that we avoid the most dangerous areas, wherein there was a high likelihood of kidnap or terrorism. Sensible advice.

Throughout both our lives, Mum has always given Pedr and I every encouragement to explore. She is a member of the Alpine Club, one of the most prestigious climbing clubs in the world. Recently she was climbing in the Himalayan mountains way up past Everest base camp, and on many other high-altitude climbs – all when over the age of eighty – and so she is not averse to a bit of risk. However, when it is your family, and the risk comes from others, then that risk is more difficult to assess or manage.

It transpired that she was not pleased about either of us going against strongly worded Foreign Office advice. She wasn't happy about Pedr's decision to go; but for me to join too was really not what she wanted (although she never said anything against our trip, and I didn't find out how much worry this had caused until after our return).

Mum's apprehensions regarding Pedr's huge cycle mirrored mine and Annwyl's. His planned trip was over 30,000 miles around the world on his own: staying in a small tent, cooking his food, and carrying all his supplies with him entirely unsupported; and on a limited budget. This gave us big concerns every day, and many an anxious wait for the latest episode of his blog. These, although interesting and fun to read, were pretty scary. At least it was good to hear he was having amazing experiences, and still going!

Pedr's obstacles and scary stories were common well before I flew out. Frozen water bottles going over the Alps; deep snow and iced-up roads; packs of mad dogs chasing his bike; isolation for many days over winter on his own . . . plus some dodgy accommodation and people to manage along the way. Every day brought more stories for all of us.

So, at least for me, I felt that I could be of some help, even if it was just for a short while. (And hopefully we could stay in the odd hotel if we found one!)

My wife on the other hand seemed positively happy that I should be venturing into these wild areas with Pedr. I tried to rationalise this by thinking that she would just do anything to support our son; rather than that she was perhaps happy to see the back of me for a few months! I suspect it was a bit of both.

Looking through my life insurance policy, though, I noticed that it would be rendered invalid if I went against British consulate advice. *Oh that's not so good,* I thought, *but no way around that one.* At least Annwyl didn't want me to go for the life insurance claim!

Anyway, we didn't talk much about the invalid insurance. We had too much else going on.

For me it was obvious: as long as I could make it, then the opportunity was just too good to miss.

Our friends, on the other hand, were just amazed that we would even consider it.

I suffered horribly at many parties, where I was the butt of all the saddle-sore jokes and nice-knowing-you quips. Annwyl's friends were aghast at her willingness to throw me to the lions on this crazy cycle, and at my age!

For work I ran a small business with two other directors. They strongly advised against attempting to try to cycle over a 4,732-metre pass with an old bike loaded up with camping gear; they doubted that I would be able to do it.

We had set the company up as a slow-growth, lifestyle-type business to fund free time for us all, but by now it was gaining lots of high-profile customers and had started growing very well. It analysed the energy usage of many large companies and drove an energy reduction plan for them. We were getting a lot of visibility and good business, so it really needed all our time.

I tried to get a satellite phone so that I could be available for business decisions from the bike. Yet this proved impossible. You are not allowed to have satellite phones in these areas of China or Pakistan without specific security clearance, and we certainly didn't need more problems when crossing the borders. We agreed a schedule of communication that I could manage over this time; as well as for me to take unpaid time away from the business, while still staying in touch.

When you are twenty-three and up for a huge challenge, conflicting sensible advice from the British consulate is just another challenge to overcome.

In reality it created the need for researching the actual situation on the ground, reading experiences of anybody else who was brave enough to spend time in these areas (not many), and balancing that against the government's advice.

Moreover, you can also use it to spur you on . . .

These are the kind of challenges that prevent most people from travelling to and experiencing these countries. The opportunity to see such restricted areas, feel the effects of their governments' policies and police on their people, and interact with those living in these countries is priceless. As a cyclist you travel slowly, yet at the same time can cover long distances; and importantly you don't present a threat or appear in any way superior. This really encourages people to interact with and talk to you.

These are the people that we all need to hear from to get a true understanding of their views, feelings, lifestyle and community, plus the pressures that affect them. Being on a bike makes you vulnerable, but it is also a really powerful way of interacting with many normal people and getting a real feel for the countries you travel through.

Pedr's argument is that if you just did everything you were supposed to do then you risk missing out on many amazing experiences in life. Furthermore, you will also miss out on meeting so many different and interesting people.

I really understood that. And anyway, Pedr had made up his mind – so that was that.

Pedr later recounted many stories of people he stayed with being really welcoming and trusting. He is connected with 'Warm

Showers' (<u>warmshowers.org</u>): a network of touring cyclists who agree to provide each other with a place to stay for a night and a meal, on the understanding that they will do the same for other travelling cyclists sometime.

One of the people Pedr stayed with in a really lovely house in Bulgaria just said to him, 'Pull the door closed behind you when you leave'. Pedr asked this man why he was so trusting. His response was, 'Well, you are on a loaded-up bicycle, travelling around the world. You can't carry much else, and you are certainly not traveling very fast'.

This puts cycle touring into great perspective, and is the root of the reward. It enables connections and facilitates interactions with everybody. We really felt that this was the door that enabled many of our best meetings and experiences together.

Supporting people who push themselves out of their comfort zone and take on major challenges, like this world tour on a bike, is really important; as they have earned all the support and encouragement of every one of us.

The most interesting and encouraging aspect of this whole experience is that almost everybody, everywhere, really loves a good story.

Most people never get the chance to have these kind of adventures, and they so much appreciate living them through you. Just by spending a little of your time with them – giving them your thoughts, passing on useful information and sharing perspectives, as well as their enjoying spending time with you – is the power of life on a bike.

It's great to get them to share their story in return, and to increase your knowledge of their village, town, or city life. It always adds a truer and honest perspective to recount later.

There is always something in common to share a laugh over, even if there is no common language.

For me, before joining Pedr, the reality was that I had very little option to back out, even if I wanted to, for fear that I would be blamed for any issue arising from his going it alone on this section.

Also, Pedr was now 7,000 miles into his trip and I couldn't resist the opportunity to have a bit of father-son time. In addition to that, mountains are my thing: I have always loved them, the Lake District being my stomping ground. And that's how, without much thought, it had been agreed that we would meet up and cycle over some of the biggest and most beautiful mountain passes in the world.

Now, on the eve of my flight to Bishkek (Kyrgyzstan) – yes, I had never heard of it either, until a few months ago – things were a bit surreal.

Packing my bike into a box, and squeezing my two pants, four socks, two shirts and one pair of trousers – in addition to my sleeping bag, tent, waterproof – into two panniers and a handlebar bag, seemed an impossible challenge.

My bike's steel frame was manufactured almost two and a half decades earlier. It was also missing front pannier fixings. I was unsure whether this was a blessing or a curse; though I did know that, if I had to ditch my pants, things may not turn out well.

My part in joining Pedr for a small portion of his huge challenge – cycling from our home in Bourne End around the world on his own, completely unsupported, with only essential water crossings by other means of travel – may seem so insignificant. But for me it was massive. How often does one get to spend eight weeks on such an adventure?! And so I was properly psyched-up, ready for the challenge.

Waiting at the airport ahead of my flight to Bishkek, I reflected on how my physical training had been thin. Preparing the business for my absence and ensuring that all the normal household jobs were up to date had taken up most of my time, and equipping my bike for the trip and trying to get as much training in as possible was really too much to do on top of that.

As far as comparable preparations for the Himalayas go, the rolling Chiltern hills are not even close – and my friends and family's awareness of this was the source of much amusement for them.

I will just have to take it easy while out there, I thought before boarding, *and it may just be that the most valuable item I am carrying will turn out to be the tow rope . . .*

Don't tell Pedr though, came the afterthought, *because he's the tow truck!*

TRAGEDY IN TAJIKISTAN

When I had arrived at Heathrow, with my bike-in-a-box and really small bags, the adventure was feeling all too real.

Rachie the check-in lady – you know, the 'been there, seen it all' type – began to stumble, having clearly never come across this situation before.

Adopting a pert position on her stool and curiosity clearly getting the better of her, she asked what was in the box. My response, 'A bicycle', was clearly not computing very well because her immediate follow-up, pitched a further few octaves higher, was, 'A bicycle in Dubai; in summer?'

Then, checking my ticket – 'Oh, where is FRU? Ah yes that'll be Bishkek, Kyrgyzstan' – the penny started to drop.

The bags garnered further attention, with 'Where's your suitcase?' and then, as if clarification was needed, 'Your bags are a bit, well, unusual'.

I enjoyed embellishing the bicycle-and-suitcase scenario; and yes, really, the panniers were all I could carry for two months – which brought a somewhat unbelieving 'Oh okay' (with a look that said *you are clearly as mad as a hatter*).

My forty-two kilogram load however was twelve kilos over the limit, and it took all my charm to reduce the excess baggage cost of £275 down to £125, claiming my carry-on bag could have been six kilograms heavier. I think she felt sorry for me.

The transfer in Dubai, from Emirates airlines to flydubai, brought another scare when upon check-in the nice lady asked how much my baggage weighed. Having fumbled for an answer, as I combined my clocking of their clearly not-so-integrated baggage systems with *Don't go and stitch yourself up* thoughts, I settled on a 'About thirty-something kilograms . . .' fib, which was so weak and feeble yet seemed to suffice. I just hoped it wouldn't tip the weights and balances of the plane too much.

Back at Heathrow, the realisation that my bike alone weighed eighteen-and-a-half kilograms had come as a bit of a shock. *Wow, they made them strong back then!* I had thought; with my subsequent reflection – *Just maybe, a newer, lighter version might have been a good investment* – coming a bit too late!

Bishkek was a surprisingly open, friendly and fun city, with kids playing happily even late into the night in the fountains, open parks, streets, and even on the wide pavements outside the parliament. The buildings there are Soviet style: squarely built and imposing, yet somehow attractive too.

It was really great to meet up with Pedr – he had been away from home for so long by that point, and we had read many scary stories of his travels to date – and it was really lovely to spend time together in Bishkek. Pedr enjoyed recovering in a decent hotel, which was a treat going from his small tent and single-burner stove. The lean, cycle-travel life had been his existence for many months by that point. He had crossed many countries, and experienced conditions varying from ice and snow in the Alps to almost 1,000 miles of vast, hot sandy desert with no shade, through Uzbekistan. It was great to see him in such high spirits, and he was so pleased to see me.

We took advantage of the city's nightlife: finding a band that was playing to enthusiastic clubgoers. The latter, of all ages, were keen to engage us in their joviality, with enthusiastic cries of 'Ypa!' (cheers in Kyrgyz) and glass-clinking celebrations. We had a really happy and fun evening.

'Cannabis Coffee', available in the hotel cafe, would have been an interesting pick-me-up drink the following morning, except that neither of us like coffee (and our Kyrgyz or Russian was clearly not good enough to get a coffee-free version).

That morning we set off for a day trip to Almaty, Kazakhstan, so that we could sort the visa stamps in the right passport for Pedr. He now had two passports, so he needed a Kyrgyzstan entry visa in his new passport – the one with the Chinese and Pakistani visas, which I had brought with me – to be as prepared as possible to cycle across the Chinese border.

The only way we could think of achieving this was to cross the border to Kazakhstan with the old passport and then go back in with the new one, as to get the inbound stamp. Crossing into China could be a challenge, we thought, since our Chinese visas were based on flights to Beijing that we'd ended up having to cancel.

Xinjiang province is the most restricted area of China, and we were aware that most tourists are refused a Chinese visa for entry across this border. Attempting to cycle over would certainly be interesting!

Pedr received some terrible news when we got back to Bishkek. Four cyclists that he had met a few weeks before in Tajikistan – two of whom he had remained in contact with – had been attacked and killed by terrorists. It was, it appeared, a random attack.

It was a tragedy for them and their families, and also sad for the lovely, welcoming and warm Tajik people, who rely on this cycle-tourist trade to supplement their basic, high-altitude subsistence living.

Pedr messaged Jay and Lauren's family members, having been one of the last people to spend time with them. Meanwhile, everybody he spoke to expressed their wish that we continued cycling through these wonderful Pamir mountains and meeting these friendly people.

Let's not, it was subsequently decided, *let these isolated yet tragic incidents stop us from travelling and getting the most out of life.*

I was incredibly pleased that we were together at that time, and could talk it through and rationalise it.

Pedr then wrote a great article about the cycling community experience and its reaction to this event, titled 'Kindred Spirits', which was published in *Cycling UK* magazine (cyclinguk.org). It's really worth a read and is available online.

OKAY DAD LET'S GET GOING

Pedr was taken by the hotel manager (ex-Kyrgyzstan special forces) to barter a personal taxi for us. Two bikes, two blokes and a twelve-hour ride, Bishkek to Osh, was agreed for 6,000 som (£60 at the time).

However, a surprise lay in store for us. This humble Honda van had wings from a jet, an engine from hell and an incredible ability to squeeze through the tiniest of gaps. VR games didn't even come close to experiencing the 'space van'. Twelve hours of adrenaline-fuelled, white-knuckle riding ensued, as it hurtled through the mountains and tunnels. Road works, red lights and oncoming traffic didn't stop us; the workmen fleeing the mad van making it perfect for a crazy Frank Spencer sketch.

We had a rest stop after about eight hours, during which our esteemed driver recommended what appeared to be a pint of milky yellowish liquid complete with brown floaters. One sip though proved way too much, and frankly it was the most disgusting thing I have ever tasted. It turned out to be horse milk, which had been left to ferment and sour in the sun. Our driver saw off two pints of it.

Sarry-Tash was the van-taxi's destination, being a little village on a three-way fork (the Tajikistan Pamir Highway one way, Osh in Kyrgyzstan another, and our route to China the third). Pedr had previously cycled through Sarry-Tash on his way to Bishkek to meet me, and so starting here made sense for us.

Our homestay had been booked through booking.com; and while different city destinations promised showers or air conditioning, ours merely boasted 'complimentary toilet paper'. Though what we hadn't realised at the time of booking was that, although sure enough we would have toilet paper, we wouldn't actually have a toilet to go with it.

Shamurat was our host and the very proud owner of the homestay. He is also a ski guide in winter, when the temperatures can be as low as minus twenty-two degrees in the day and as far down as minus thirty-five at night. We felt glad to be there in the summer.

The view from the homestay was truly spectacular, with three peaks over 7,000 metres seemingly all within touching distance. The most well-known of the three, called Lenin, was apparently one of the easier peaks to climb.

We set off from the homestay with forty-five-kilogram bikes, which included plenty of water, for a 'gentle introduction' cycle to ease me into the world of cycle touring. It turned out to be a 1,000-metre climb, eventually reaching a peak of 3,773 metres before a proper switchback road to get to the Chinese border some forty-five miles away.

Well . . . I was not used to a heavy bike, nor climbing one up 1,000 metres: especially at ridiculous heights, where the air is thinner than a mosquito's whisker and lots more panting than usual is required to power those pedals.

Sarry-Tash Homestay

Sarry-Tash Peter and Pedr

The views compensated handsomely though; the most spectacular mountain scenery becoming even more jagged and snowy as we headed towards the Chinese border.

Brewing up and taking in the sights of
the border mountains to China

By this time I was completely knackered, and the 'shipping container hotel' we knew was somewhere nearby seemed heaven-sent. No showers, toilet or toilet paper were promised this time either, but that hadn't seemed to matter in my state of exhaustion.

We were to be disappointed, though, because the shipping container was fully booked! And so, as it started raining, we had to resort to putting the tent up in the only flat ground around – the local dump!

Some 'gentle introduction'! I thought, followed by *China here we come!*

Kyrgyzstan–China border camp site
Cooking breakfast porridge at 7:00 before crossing into China.
Yes, it was cold!

MADE IT TO XINJIANG

We started on our quest to enter China at eight a.m., as soon as the border opened. All our paperwork was in order, complete with valid Chinese and Pakistani visas in new passports, plus now all the necessary stamps courtesy of our detour to Almaty, Kazakhstan.

It had been necessary for Pedr to get a second passport because he had been cycling with his original one across much of Central Europe, Serbia, Romania, Bulgaria, Turkey, Georgia, Uzbekistan and Tajikistan before arriving in Kyrgyzstan to meet me. This had taken him seven months, and meanwhile I had needed his passport in order to get his Pakistani and Chinese visas, both of which took many weeks to sort out. It goes without saying that he couldn't be without his passport on his journey, and so we'd had to source him a second one.

The distance between the Kyrgyzstan border exit post and the Chinese border entry post (where you finally receive your entry stamp), is 147km.

Between the two we were forced to get a taxi, along with being subjected to a total of nine separate army and police checks, each of which insisted on scanning both our passports and most of our bodily parts (faces, fingers, thumbs); two X-rays; and one complete 3D body scan.

Oh . . . and not forgetting multiple take-everything-out episodes, along with our phones and laptops being taken away. We subsequently discovered that all our devices had been blocked, with our details downloaded onto their servers. So, with no further access to the internet or data services, our phones were now effectively useless in China.

It was quite an ordeal: us thinking we could be rejected at any time, which would have meant completely changing our plans. Yet luck was on our side, and we seemed to be reacting in the right way to the numerous intimidating shouts directed at us in different languages from the guards. I think it must have been a test to see if we actually did understand any of the local languages – they really didn't want us talking to their people.

While we didn't have anything to hide, it was nevertheless a huge intrusion to have all one's personal (and some of their business') data being downloaded and kept on a Chinese server somewhere. We expected this to be the case, though, and just knew that in order to get across the border we just had to go along with each demand.

Between the border posts, in no man's land, it was unsurprisingly deserted – and beautiful. Here's a picture I took midway. In it the red and grey rocks make a lovely contrast (I studied Geology many years ago so found it super interesting), though I was clearly not going to be able to get any closer.

Finally, almost nine hours later, we managed to clear the border. We were excited to finally be cycling in China. By now it was four-thirty p.m., and with over 100km to cycle to Kashgar we decided to stay in the weird border town village of Ulugqat.

Beautiful geology and mountains in no man's land towards China
Taken on the 147km forced taxi ride between Kyrgyzstan exit
border and China entry point

The first place we cycled past that looked like a tourist hotel had a lot of heavily armed guards, with a unit set ready for confrontation. We were aware of recent violent clashes between the police and the native Uyghur population, and the attempt by the government to 'encourage' Han Chinese to settle in the area. The streets were quiet and there was tension in the air. We continued cycling until we got to the centre of the town and came across another tourist hotel.

We checked in to this hotel – the only one that would take us – and in the process once again had our bodies and luggage scanned, plus our passports taken away.

We did, however, find a little local restaurant and had our best meal to date. It was also the only restaurant with any locals in – all the others being deserted.

We had no chance of understanding the menu, and since Google Translate was not working – surprise, surprise! – we just made eating gestures and pointed to other people's food. About the only thing we could understand in the restaurant were the smiley icons denoting the cleanliness ratings, and in this respect it had the worst score – a red sad face!

Restaurant in Ulugqat showing cleanliness rating – red sad face!

THE CHASE TO KASHGAR

The old road was being repaired and was shut, so we hit the highway's hard shoulder as the only other way to Kashgar.

After the second police checkpoint and a collaborative chat involving translation tools and six police officers of differing rank, we were politely informed that the smaller road would be safer for us, and that we were to be escorted to that road. They wanted to put our bikes in their truck but we refused, asking if we could just follow their vehicle.

After some negotiations they agreed, and we set off.

However, when we stopped for lunch, another police car had spotted us, and as we were eating a group of five officers came into the restaurant. They had bulletproof vests, batons and machine guns, and asked to see passports and visas. With them being clearly unhappy with our presence, and much tut-tutting on our part, we endured more scans of our passports, and more questions, before they took photos of us eating and then left.

The restaurant owner was pleased to see us, and the locals were all-smiles and encouraging, although sadly we had no common language. Their son did, though, then retrieve an unusual instrument, starting to play and sing to us. How lovely that was.

Restaurant stop, Ulugqat to Kashgar

All was okay until we left the restaurant. The officers were still there, sat in their police car waiting for us.

From there we were followed by a series of police cars – five in total – all the way to the Kashgar checkpoint about fifty miles away, which proved useful for directions at least. At that point we were handed over to their forces at the city checkpoint. It's pretty weird being followed by police cars with their lights flashing all that way at bike speed. We were a bit conspicuous!

Heading into Kashgar, on the road for bikes and mopeds, the traffic was getting busier by the mile; until we joined the scrum at the lights and crossings for some who-dares-wins dodgems, which was actually quite fun.

As we cycled into Kashgar we met another Chinese tourist, who recommended a hostel that proved to be both good and cheap. Eight to a bedroom, one toilet and shower between us proved a bit of a challenge – though not as much as the legendary Chinese snoring. Fortunately we were pretty tired, and with some local beer and a decent bed sleep came easily.

Kashgar is one of the oldest continuously inhabited cities in the world.

Its position as one of the largest cities in the middle of the political, religious and way-of-life difference between the Chinese-populace Han and the local Chinese Islamic Uyghur population made it a city of contrasts and challenge, with overt displays of tension, power and control clearly a big part of everyday life for its inhabitants.

Recent violent clashes between them have decimated some of Kashgar Old Town. There is now a stark contrast between the Old Town's (lovely) remaining buildings and the newer concrete-block replacements.

The city mosque still stands and is really worth a visit, being a particularly beautiful and poignant reminder of the tensions and way-of-life differences between these groups. Strangely, there is also a museum for the Uyghur traditional culture and artefacts. Although it's great that they preserve this heritage, it also imparts a strange (and political) notion that the Uyghur way of life is historic and the Han way of life the future. I am not sure if that's how everybody else felt, but it was difficult to ignore.

Kashgar Old Town and new buildings

We visited the tourist information shop and wrote our first, and only, postcards home. We also shipped home some of the unnecessary cold weather and duplicate kit that we had (I had brought some better and lighter pans and plates to reduce the overall weight, so we sent back their previous counterparts). This would make a big difference to our weight as we started going up into the big mountain ranges.

Kashgar had two vibrant markets, both very different: one a very tidy and smart fruit-and-street-food-based market, and the other a cattle market just out of town. The cattle market was busy and dynamic, if a little more brutal than western equivalents, but was clearly an important and active community trading centre. The fruit and street food market by comparison was great to visit, and the cleanliness and presentation was helped kept in line by the constant attention of the local police force.

Kashgar's fruit and street food market

We were always aware of the vast numbers of police present everywhere. A few times I counted the number of police that I could see at any one point in time, and it was usually more than five. This was strange for us and begged the question *Why so many?*

I am sure anybody trying to steal anything would not make it more than ten steps without getting boshed on the head by one of them. It's more like an activist mob checking your every move; I could imagine them checking to see if I had brushed my teeth that morning, like your mum did when you were five.

Early one morning we walked out of our hostel in central Kashgar to find all of the shopkeepers lined up in rows, chanting, and being 'encouraged' to loudly acclaim allegiance to the Chinese leader Xi Jinping, all the while surrounded by police dressed in body armour and carrying riot shields and long wooden batons.

(We had of course not understood the shopkeepers' words, yet were told by other people staying in the hostel that that was what they were saying.)

When we tried to capture an image of this strange event, some of the shopkeepers tried hard to catch our eye and, gesturing towards the police guards, implied that we really shouldn't take pictures.

Kashgar police and shopkeepers

ON THE RUN FROM
THE CHINESE POLICE

After a few days exploring Kashgar we set off along the road out of the city and towards the mountains.

Long, straight road out of Kashgar. Stopping for lunch on the Karakoram Highway G314 on our way to the mountains

All went well until we were stopped at the first checkpoint, ten miles down the road. Here we were escorted for questioning.

Eventually they got an English speaker on the phone, who asked how many hours it would take us to get to Tashkurgan, the border town with Pakistan.

Well, that took us by surprise.

'It's about one hundred and eighty-five miles and over several 4,000-metre passes through the Karakoram mountains, so about ninety hours I guess.'

A pause at their end. Then,

'Well, you need to plan your route very carefully. Where are you staying?'

We knew the only correct answer to this was 'In the "tourist hotels"', since they are the only places you can stay.

In reality, everybody knew that this was impossible. There was only one tourist hotel en route – a Yurt – and we needed at least four days to get to the border.

We were then informed that it is illegal to camp in China. They became quite serious and threatened us, saying that if we were caught camping they would 'teach us to obey the Chinese laws'.

Our adventure had now just presented us with an impossible challenge, and set in motion a game of cat and mouse that we really didn't want with the Chinese police force. Our clearest options were either to cancel our planned trip, cycle continuously for ninety hours without sleeping, or to go as fast as we could and rest wherever possible in the hope of not being seen.

We did our very best to stick to the laws of this new land, and to go along with all the personal searches and close monitoring of our every move. There is palpable tension in everyday life here: not just for us, but particularly for the locals – and especially the native Uyghurs.

At the first checkpoint leaving Kashgar a guard discovered Pedr's Leatherman bicycle repair multi-tool (a knife, pliers and allen key combined) in one of his bags. They tried very hard to confiscate it.

We had other ideas.

Pedr kicked up a big fuss, saying it was the only toolset we had for the bikes, and that we really needed it. As the 'discussions' escalated, the local Chinese people started telling us not to anger the guards and that it is illegal to carry a knife. They were clearly concerned for us, even though our request was quite reasonable.

A farmer behind us had a good-sized hand scythe for his vegetables – if that was okay then so surely was our small Leatherman?! The locals too were in quite vocal support of the guard, though I suspect that this was more to do with them being required to be seen to support him, rather than the much larger risk of supporting us. They were genuinely scared on our behalf.

After a series of escalations through every rank at the large checkpoint we eventually got to keep it. *Phew! Another close shave.* We would have been particularly vulnerable without it as we ventured into the high Karakoram and Himalayan mountains. A broken bike in the mountains would be a disaster; and, regardless of that, we used the Leatherman all the time.

Their face-scanning and passport-checking software was either not conditioned to beards or to British features, I don't know which, but we both kept failing the checks. This was to the obvious frustration of the guards, who were clearly powerless to override the automated computer systems.

Anyhow, the challenge had been set. One hundred and eighty-five miles to cover, several 4,000-metre passes to negotiate, and nowhere to stay. Man against system.

It was about this time that we discovered the camera gantries. These – positioned every couple of miles, with twelve cameras per gantry; six either side – tracked our every move. *Ah okay, so this is how they would find us.* Our bikes not making very good getaway vehicles, added to active camera monitoring like this, made our challenge seemingly impossible. The BBC reported in 2017 that there were 170 million cameras in Xinjiang province.

With every village also came another police car and checkpoint, for yet another 'passport scan and questioning' session. They stopped everybody, so it was not just us. One of the policemen who spoke some English kindly asked if we were elite cycling athletes. I guess he was trying to convince himself we could get to Tashkurgan before nightfall.

I really didn't look much like an elite anything other than an exhausted, crazy dude on a bike; but hey, I can take a compliment!

As the cycling got to mid-afternoon, and because we needed to find somewhere to stay, things got more interesting. We were desperate not to pick up another police tail otherwise we may be cycling all night. Likewise, given their promise to teach us to obey the Chinese laws, we had visions of being introduced to their educational correctional facilities, and so that was on our mind!

We stopped for a late lunch in a little village of about twenty shops and restaurants. In the scorching heat of the day each owner had on a bulletproof vest, and held a riot shield and a long wooden club. In the middle of nowhere. The vests were marked 'Police', and there was an odd atmosphere.

It made for quite a strange lunch stop. They were clearly unsettled that we were here, and were quite limited in their interaction. We plucked up courage to ask whether there was anywhere we could stay for the night?

'Em . . . No . . .' was how to best interpret their response; their appearing surprised that we should even ask. Nobody would give us accommodation here.

So how could we beat the cameras, bypass the police checkpoint at the end of the village, and also find ourselves somewhere to spend the night without getting caught? This wasn't going to be easy.

We decided that the first thing to do was for me to stay at the restaurant while Pedr quietly left and scouted the area for good hiding places for the night.

Our best idea up to then was to trick the camera system. And so when Pedr returned we left the village on our bikes, waving a public goodbye to the shop owners, passing back through the checkpoint and past several camera gantries – so the cameras and checkpoint both caught us going out of the village – before then going off the road. At that point we doubled back: through the bush, fields and hedges (keeping away, as we did, from the road, cameras and police checkpoint), all the way to the place behind the village that Pedr had found earlier. When there, we found ourselves close to and behind the shops once more, but now well out of sight.

Settling in at nightfall, we suffered numerous scares: men shouting when they heard the noise from us putting up our tent; dogs barking menacingly; lights scanning across the tent (later found to be lightning); and a police truck with flashers on passing up and down the gravel track we had come along through the middle of the night.

We could see and hear that the focus of activity was at the building site a mile or so up the road. This was near where we had left the road, and so it did not make for a good night's sleep. They gave up looking for us at about two a.m.

Resting place for the first night from Kashgar, heading for the Karakoram mountains

We broke camp at four a.m. and headed up the road. Fortunately the police checkpoint guards were asleep in their chairs outside, and we cycled quietly past. Just maybe they were as tired as we were, so we got away with it.

Cycling from the flat plains out of Kashgar we proceeded to climb 998 metres (covering thirty-three miles as we did) with no sleep. That was enough for me that day!

The road began winding its way up into the Karakoram mountains and away from the long straight roads near Kashgar. It was reassuring to see 'G314' on the signpost: it meant we were on the right road. Not that I doubted Pedr's GPS navigation skills!

Heading into the Karakoram mountains on the G314

Higher into the Karakoram mountains

The surface was smooth tarmac and recently built tunnels and well-built viaducts gave us an even ride on very-well-maintained roads. There was however very little space for cyclists through said tunnels, and the trucks were squeezing past way too close for comfort.

Bright sunshine gave way to cloudy skies and menacingly stormy conditions as we climbed higher and nearer the rugged mountains; so we started looking for somewhere, once again, to hide for the night.

We discovered a small shed – locked up, but on a ledge up the mountainside. It had a little area, just out of sight of the road, in which we could fit the tent, and so was a great place to get some well-earned sleep.

We dragged the bikes up and laid them against the back of the shed, also out of sight. Moreover, we were in the mountains now, and so would be harder to find.

The trusty tent provided great shelter from another major thunderstorm. I am used to big storms when up in the mountains, but this one was truly epic. The extent of the rain, thunder and lightning felt like even the gods were after us.

The tent though was superb, and we were so very tired that the thunder just rocked us off to sleep, and even the sound of police cars (with their flashing lights, passing up and down through the night) seemed less menacing. We knew they wouldn't find us here.

The next morning the thunderstorm had passed, yet we woke to find the whole Karakoram Highway blocked by a massive landslide. Bulldozers were hard at work clearing up the mess and eventually opened up a single lane as to allow us through. As we did so we passed two trucks that were partially covered and completely stuck in mud and rocks. Boy I was glad we hadn't been caught up in that.

Trucks stuck in the landslide that blocked the Karakoram Highway

Before long, the sky cleared and an area of mountains and lakes opened up as the road stopped its inexorable ascent to a lovely high plateau – and some much-appreciated easy cycling!

Muztagata is an impressive 7,546-metre mountain. It's the second highest of the mountains which form the northern edge of the Tibetan Plateau. As we arrived at the lake the sky cleared its cloud cap to reveal beautiful glaciers feeding down to our road as we cycled around its base. And what a beautiful way it was to spend my fifty-sixth birthday.

Yet staying somewhere that night was once again going to prove tricky. We had reached a beautiful lake, on its own a big local attraction, and the police were out in force, as were the Chinese tourists.

Beautiful high plateau, lakes and mountains, and a little relief from the long climb

Muztagata Mountain: 7,546 metres high, with glaciers feeding a beautiful turquoise lake

The lake itself was sealed off, with both barbed wire and guards present. The mountains to either side were *huge*, which meant our only possibility was to scramble and push the bikes away from the lake and up steep rubble hills before it got too late, and hope we were not spotted.

We decided to be safe and go over two hills' distance from the lake before hiding the bikes and trying to be as inconspicuous as possible in the hot sun before it gradually went behind the mountain. Soon enough, though, we spotted a drone scouting the area beyond the first hill. We stayed down, out of sight. It gave up after a tense thirty minutes: during which, luckily for us, it didn't scan over our side of the second hill. We were unsure as to whether this was a police or a citizen drone (but, given that the citizens there were most likely to inform the police, it perhaps didn't much matter).

We had found a lovely place to stay, overlooking the mountains and the lake, but as we started getting off to sleep we heard a group of people. They were, it seemed, walking in line together in the middle of the night. By now we were unsure whether paranoia was setting in or if the police really were trying that hard to find us. Either way we managed to escape yet another night intact while 'on the run'.

(I use that term because we were supposed to register where we were staying each evening with the local police. Though we were clearly unable to do that at present, as in the mountains there were no villages or hotels or police stations to report to!)

Awaiting us the next morning was another tough 4,000-metre climb: this time with some very inquisitive camels. Even more curious, it turned out, were the Chinese tourists: following me up the hill in their car, video recorder poking out of the window; zooming in to record my struggles.

Well, I hope they enjoyed my pain!

*Camels and mountains as we started
the climb over the next high pass*

*Final summit at 4,000 metres, before descending
thirty miles to Tashkurgan*

The past few days had been really tough, mentally and physically; and, in the aftermath of the climb, as we descended for the thirty or so miles between there and Tashkurgan, I was exhausted, thirsty and hungry. We had run out of food and water and, in the scorching heat, were on the verge of finding the nearest policeman and asking for some water. In our situation that really would have been the last resort, and we narrowly managed to avoid it – as just then we found a small local restaurant and indulged in some much-needed drinks plus food.

Refreshed, we started the relatively short and a far less-stressful ten-mile ride to Tashkurgan, where upon our arrival we checked into a real tourist hotel. Immediately the on-duty clerk did as required and registered us with the police.

We were now expecting to get a police visit, and with it a grilling about why we hadn't checked in for the past three nights, as well as where we *did* stay. Our only hope was that maybe they wouldn't want to expose their failed efforts to find us, or perhaps that they would now just be happy we were out of the Uyghur-populated areas. We hoped this would be the case, as we were almost free!

Pedr and I had got our story straight, should we be questioned by the police. We had agreed to say that we had just cycled all the time and only stopped to eat and rest (*not camp*). That was of course perfectly within the law – albeit pretty much impossible to do. You really did need shelter in those mountains at night, and so a tent was required. (A tent would also have been required by every other mountaineer scaling Chinese mountains, and so I am not sure how that works for them either?!)

The constant chasing, hassling, monitoring and polite intim-idation of the past few days was taking its toll. And it was good that there were two of us to experience this together and keep one another going.

One cannot begin to understand the impact on the local population living with this intense, overbearing and intimidatory control. How they survive with all this monitoring and intrusive invasion in their lives, I just cannot imagine. I am not surprised that, whenever possible, they do everything they can to change their situation and tell the world about this unreasonable level of control.

We later found out, from a fellow biker on an online forum, how he was forced to pack up his makeshift camp and cycle, and was subsequently followed by a police car for as long as it took to get to the next tourist hotel – which, in our case, would have been a *really long way*. The poor chap recounted to us how he was made to continue cycling through the night, when he was completely exhausted and returned back to Kashgar.

The looming threat of teaching us to obey the Chinese laws had to us seemed targeted more towards their 'educational' correction facilities. We hadn't given this too much thought at the time; although, some months later after my return home, I saw a documentary on these very same centres. It made extremely disturbing viewing, and left me feeling incredibly pleased that we had managed to avoid getting to experience them personally.

Every business in the area appeared to have a riot shield, body armour and a long wooden club visible and immediately available at all times. And this hotel was no exception.

When we found them by the desk, unattended, the temptation to play was too great. Yet although fun was had, I think the hotel staff would have had a huge sense-of-humour failure if we had been caught!

Pedr with the hotel's riot shield and baton

That evening, in our hotel room in Tashkurgan, we received a call asking for us to come down to reception.

We had anticipated that the police would start asking questions, and so it was not unexpected – but still it was concerning.

Fortunately, this turned out to be a call from the tourist information office in Kashgar. They had somehow tracked us down to this hotel, and were phoning to inform us that they should have charged us more for a parcel we had sent home through them. They were, they said, going to add the difference our hotel bill.

That was not great on two counts. Firstly, once we had paid for postage then surely they could not suddenly change the price later on. Secondly – and far more concerning – was that they had somehow tracked us down to this hotel.

We politely stated that since we had agreed a price for the parcel it was not reasonable to ask for more money at a later date. And although they did finally acquiesce, I admit to having had a little guilty concern for the person who had charged us in Kashgar – as maybe they would be forced to make up the difference from their wages.

We took a few days to recover following our arduous cycle, ahead of our upcoming departure from China.

Tashkurgan is the border town to Pakistan – even though it is one hundred miles from the crossing itself! – and the only way to enter Pakistan from there is by bus. (We tried to find how we could possibly cycle across the border, but, despite our best efforts, it became clear that this was simply not possible.)

Our hotel's reception staff spoke a little English, and we thought they would be able to help us arrange our travel to the border. We had three pretty simple questions, which we put to them.

'When does the bus go to Pakistan?'

'Every day.'

'Where can we get cash?'

'There is nowhere to get cash. We can exchange some for you.'

'Where is the best place to eat?'

'There are no good restaurants. Eat at the hotel.'

All three of the answers they gave turned out to be wrong. We found a cash machine around the corner; the bus didn't operate on the weekend; and there were much better restaurants nearby.

It was strange how they answered these questions politely and with total confidence, yet must have known that said answers were incorrect. I assumed that they were trying to do what they could to get us to stay in the hotel and to use their services, and possibly they were unaware of the bus schedule, though that did feel unlikely.

It's quite strange to think of a border crossing that has a no man's land in between which is itself hundreds of kilometres long and a hundred kilometres wide. That just seems like a huge waste of good land and space.

Though we could see why there would be good reason, for at least the Uyghur people, to get out of China, so I guess this was one of their defenses to enable their forces enough time to react and retrieve wannabe escapees.

Tashkurgan itself is really a town serving a disparate farming community. The locals run small subsistence farms and come to the town for the market and basic necessities. There are few luxuries there.

Our hotel was clean, and had the appearance of being luxurious, though the quality of workmanship relating to the general building and its maintenance was still very poor by our accustomed standards. Nevertheless the hotel *looked* great; and, compared to the other buildings, it was clearly the best in town. We would have very few opportunities to stay in 'good' accommodation, so I had been happy to treat us both when this opportunity arose. The hotel was also surrounded by fences, barbed wire and big gates that were guarded night and day, and it seemed odd that they felt the need to protect the hotel in this way. It was unclear who they were protecting. I guess it was to stop the locals, who were mostly very poor subsistence farmers, from disrupting life at the 'swanky' hotel.

We were advised to visit a Pakistani restaurant, as it was said to be one of the best in town. Indeed, the food was *excellent* – in fact, I'd go as far as to say it was one of the tastiest meals I have ever had. It was yak stew, and the meat was tender and well-spiced. I quite like a lot of fresh spices, and was surprisingly excited to think that there could be more yak stews to come as we cycled through Pakistan.

It was such a treat to have this experience on the back of what had, for the past four days, been a very lean diet. We had been surviving on the basic dry food we had in our bags; this limited by what we could carry on our bikes and cook up in the mountains on a single-burner stove. We certainly needed to get our energy back and eat some good food.

The Pakistani owner of the restaurant was very welcoming, and he was telling us how much of a challenge it was to set up shop in China. He said that you don't get many businesses or goods crossing over from Pakistan to China. His customers were mostly non-Chinese visitors, people passing through, and students from Pakistan. He was very pleased to see us and spent time sitting in conversation, despite having a busy restaurant. He was eager to hear about our journey, though it was only later on that we would understand why.

HIGHEST PAVED BORDER CROSSING IN THE WORLD

As our bus went over the Khunjerab Pass the relief was palpable and genuine. It is weirdly stressful to be watched and monitored so closely by everybody around you all the time – police, citizens, cameras, and even drones – while you just try to have a holiday.

We were clearly not the only ones who felt that a huge weight had been lifted, as the atmosphere on the bus went from sternly quiet to party-like: with cheers and whoops of delight and tension-relief as we crossed the border. The Chinese guard, however, went into a proper sulk, immediately grabbing the Tannoy to reassert his authority. *I am in charge here until you get off,* I imagine his utterances translated to, *so you better behave!*

It was quite interesting to see the guard's reaction when his Chinese state authority evaporated at the border, thereby removing his power. He became further unsettled, and resorted to behaviour that was even more irrational and overtly assertive.

For instance (and much to our consternation), he would not allow the bus to stop until it reached the Pakistani village of Sost, which is located some fifty miles from the border and 2,532 metres below the pass. It would have been amazing to ourselves cycle to Sost down this road.

Pedr and I really wanted to cycle as much of the route as possible, so we vowed, when we got to Sost, to cycle back up to the Khunjerab Pass where our bus had travelled and then back down to Sost again, despite the huge effort required. As such the plan was to take two days to cycle back up and down again, staying on the Pakistan side of the border and camping when we were tired.

After waking up in Sost the next day, we set out to do just that. But after just twenty miles, and only five hundred metres higher up than Sost, the Pakistan border guards wouldn't't let us continue that day – their reasoning being that we couldn't camp above the checkpoint.

What's more, we needed a permit to even camp where we were – which we didn't have – so they then tried to send us back to Sost!

Well, we really didn't want to do that. The discussions were escalated all the way to the chief of border police . . . who was not happy for us to camp near his border control post.

Furthermore, the National Park guard also refused to let us stay without a permit. Upon further pressing, though, he did agree to let us stay, though only if the chief of border police took responsibility for us. Which of course he would not do.

By now our plight was being heard by every single individual at the border area, and just then I was approached by a notably shady-looking tough guy, who pulled me to one side. We could stay with him, he said, in his big stone building at the side of the road. What's more, he added, we were not to worry about what the chief of police nor the national park guard said – they didn't matter! *He* was in control here. This man turned out to be the army commander for the region.

Well then, nothing could go wrong with this scenario. Except that the chief of border police had our passports, and he didn't look very happy with either the commander or this scenario.

We thought it was better to use all our diplomatic skills to get everybody onside, so with a long round of shuttle diplomacy we reached an agreement whereby everybody was happy, and we could stay . . . phew!

We had translation help from a local NGO figure, and this man just kept mumbling 'It's all messed up, it's all messed up', much to our amusement. It may well have been messed up . . . but at least we got to stay.

We now had 1,732 metres of climbing and eighty-two miles of steep winding roads to cover that day in order to reach the top of the pass and then return back to Sost before sunset, else the police would be chasing us again. This was going to be the biggest cycle day of my life by a long way.

This was a huge moment for us, and one of the highlights of our trip. We managed to cycle all the way up the pass, several days after driving down it in the bus.

We had a beautiful but very hard cycle, and as we finally reached the top we were absolutely mobbed. Purely coincidentally it was Pakistan Independence Day: the anniversary of Pakistan's gaining its sovereignty from the UK in 1947. It was a national holiday there and the road was full of happy people taking a trip to the border. They were all very pleased to see us, and we spent a long time at the top talking to everybody and being photographed – so much so that I started to really get cold and shivery. We still had a very long (but at least downhill) run back, and therefore needed to get going.

Switchback road descending to Sost
This was one of the flatter sections of the highway, showing the river
valley the road wound across for miles. Super tarmac, and a mostly
smooth road, made for great cycling

A Pakistani TV company was filming at the top and requested an interview. After we had said yes, they started by asking what we thought of the food In Pakistan. We had just arrived over the border, we said, and so were only able to compare the great yak stew with the rather dull backpacking food we had while climbing the Karakoram mountains in China. Immediately thereafter they changed tack, and started asking why we were here and what did we think. We gave a 'happy to be here' message, and as soon as we mentioned that Pedr was travelling around the world on his bike they became really interested. (Indeed, this subject would prove such a hit with so many different people along our route, to the extent that we would start looking for quiet places to stop, rather than busy ones that would likely bring with them big delays and countless selfie requests.)

China–Pakistan border Khunjerab Pass
Here we were at the Khunjerab Pass. At 4,732 metres it is the
highest paved international border crossing in the world, marking
the official border between China and Pakistan

Pedr wrote an article about our trip up these big mountains, published by Treadlie (treadlie.com.au). Its title was 'Bikes on Big Mountains' and it featured a picture of me, struggling up these winding roads and vast mountain landscapes, taken on our way to the Khunjerab Pass.

Cycling back down was exhilarating. Over 2,000 metres of descent on these long smooth roads was such a great feeling, and made up for the tortuously slow upward journey. We were tired, though, and I could tell that my blood sugar level was markedly low. On one section, near a bridge, the road had slipped and in doing so opened up a large gap in the tarmac across the entire width of the road. I was travelling way too fast to stop in time; and, reaching the gap, I managed to jump the front wheel to avoid going head over heels, yet as a result of doing so hit the rough section hard, causing my front bag to rip off my bike and bounce on the road in front of me – where I couldn't avoid then running over it. I somehow managed to stay on the bike, skidding sideways to a very wobbly halt. Yet the dislodged front bag was the one with our valuables and breakables in it, and so this was not looking good. Amazingly enough, though, after straightening the bag, its contents – including my phone, on which I was writing the notes of this trip, and Pedr's camera – were all unharmed. I could have been quite badly hurt, and we could have lost both our phones and cameras.

Descending back to Sost
It was getting late as we descended the final miles. The sun disappeared behind the mountains and the cold mountain air caused us to wrap up again

After continuing down at a slower pace, we finally got back to our crumbling 'Asia Star Hotel' room late that night. This was to the relief of the owner, who – bless him – was very concerned about us. He gave us a great meal and we just crashed out.

Sost is an interesting town, being the drop-off point for goods that have been loaded onto the very pretty, dressed-up goods trucks that are commonplace in Pakistan. Each driver takes huge pride in their truck: painting them in bright colours and adding all sorts of dangly and shiny objects. Some of these are for good luck.

Painted truck in Pakistan

By comparison the typical British truck is boring and corporate; being generally owned and run by large transport companies, rather than individuals resultantly taking pride in their largest business asset.

Talking to the locals, the goods traffic here is expected to grow substantially in the coming decade, with China having also recently pledged to do their best to keep the pass open all year round.

Strategically, the Karakoram Highway is of very significant value to China. It is the fastest route to access the shipping lanes from the Arabian Sea via the deep-water port of Karachi, as well as the Pakistan International Container Terminal, Gwadar Port and Port Qasim. These all have easy access and close proximity to the oil-rich states via the Gulf of Oman, as well as granting good access to the Suez Canal for shipments to and from Europe and the West.

It is not surprising that China has invested heavily in the development and maintenance of this highway, nor also that it upholds a good relationship with Pakistan. They have even named the Karakoram Highway the 'friendship highway' as an indicator of the positive relations between the two neighbours.

In Sost we saw a small school bus careering through the town in the morning: a number of school-age children packed inside, as well as a handful of them on the roof rack – all hanging on, laughing, as the bus lurched along the rough road. It was great to see so many happy children clearly enjoying the ride, though it also looked as if some of them would fall off at any moment, and appeared extremely dangerous to our eyes!

If this was back in the UK, there would be a large outcry of horror; it would make headline news and a full-on enquiry would be launched.

I should add, for context, that my wife is a very good and very experienced primary school teacher. (Yes, I would have to say that – but it is true!) I know just how hard she works to combat this protected and often spoilt lifestyle of a lot of British children by taking them outdoors as much as possible, and integrating the teaching of all subjects – Maths, English, Music, etc. – with coordination and socialisation through play. The kids love it and learn much faster this way, and naturally take part in group sports. She, as do a lot of other teachers, fights a daily battle against a tide of bureaucratic paperwork and rules and restrictions. These all have the laudable objectives of keeping children safe and monitoring their progress, yet also restrict the freedom and spontaneity of opportunities, and critically take away teachers' valuable time completing the necessary paperwork.

That said, the balance in Sost does appear to be way too dangerous!

China provides a lot of the telecoms, internet, camera technology and its management for Pakistan. I couldn't help thinking that this was a bit of a risk for the country's sovereignty, i.e. whereby so much of their infrastructure is being supplied and managed by their neighbour. Though I guess the strategic importance of the Karakoram Highway to China is good collateral for ensuring continued positive relations, as well as potentially offsetting some of this risk. Moreover the economy and basic electricity supply in Pakistan is clearly in a poor state, and so any assistance I am sure is gratefully received.

When we raised this ostensible overreliance with the locals, they seemed oblivious to the dangers of control through abuse of this type of technology. They were just pleased to have better infrastructure, roads and power support from China, and were quick to point out the close and positive relationship they share.

We witnessed many power cuts in Sost, which the locals seemed to accept as normal occurrences. Indeed, such shortages were required in order to share out the available power among the villages and cities in the region.

Imran Khan had at the time recently been appointed as the new prime minister of Pakistan, and was hugely supported by the general population. The prevailing feeling of the community was that the previously corrupt government officials were now being removed, and a big positive change was in progress: one that would be good for the country and its general population.

Many people we spoke to were pleasantly surprised that I had indeed heard of Imran Khan, and knew of him as an excellent cricketer and captain, having often seen him play against England.

This positive view of Pakistan, together with our interesting stories about their beautiful mountains and the upbeat, friendly attitude of almost everybody we came across, was really valued by the locals. They expressed concern that a lot of the international media were portraying an unreasonably negative view of their country and people, and so much appreciated this positive reflection. Not only that, but they greatly encouraged us to talk about it when we got home!

We were pretty exhausted after the ride back up to the Chinese border, and so agreed to take it easy and to enjoy a leisurely cycle through the Hunza Valley for the next few days.

We had by now managed without milk for many weeks: the impossibility of keeping milk from going sour when on the bikes meaning carrying it was not really an option. Even dried powder ends up as a sticky lump, plus that sour horse milk we had sampled in Kyrgyzstan was still 'fresh' in our memory. They generally serve milk tea in Pakistan – I guess they inherited that from the British prior to 1947 – and so this suddenly seemed novel to us, despite its being an everyday staple back home in Britain.

On the subject of food and drink, the Eid fast period had now started. This 'Feast of Sacrifice' took on a whole new meaning, and provided us with a huge shock when, at about seven a.m., we rounded one particular bend. We were now heading down a straight road on which there were three cows – spaced out one after the other: each at the edge of the road, their legs trussed up, and with entire families sat atop them – having their main throat arteries cut open.

We had to cycle through the blood that was running down the road. It was just so unexpected and extraordinary, and frankly quite shocking.

When I returned home I spoke to a distinguished teaching vet friend of my family's about this. His response was, 'Well that's what we used to do on farms in the UK all the time, not so many years ago. It's only recently that we have introduced the controls and requirements governing animal slaughter.

I guess it was just a shock to come across it like that.

As we descended through the Hunza Valley, and got further away from the mountains, we noticed that the food menu had also changed. First up, and much to my disappointment, we could no longer get yak stew.

They were also, we were informed, at the end of the apricot season, and small delicious apples had replaced apricots as the available fruit. Indeed, when we discussed this with the locals they just expected that the availability of food was dependent on its availability within their immediate community. They didn't expect food to be transported very far, or kept available out of season.

Back home, by contrast, large-scale food production, deep cold storage and year-round crop production has largely replaced seasonal availability. The cost to pay for this though is increased food prices and complex supply chains that need to be maintained and managed.

Before we came to Pakistan we really didn't have much of an expectation or understanding of the people or landscape. What we now found was so far removed from all of our arbitrary presumptions and (by extension) limited expectations, and so *amazingly beautiful*, that it was an all-round wonderful surprise and reassuringly positive experience.

We cycled into Passu that evening. Passu was a lovely green village, with lots of fruit trees, and the locals kept giving us their summer apples and apricots. It also boasted a truly awe-inspiring mountain, often referred to as 'Passu Cathedral' or 'Passu Cones'; along with large glaciers; green meadows by the lake; and super-friendly, welcoming people. We had a truly amazing time here and were invited to stay in a room in one of their houses.

'Passu Cathedral' mountain

Peter and Pedr climbing in the mountains over Passu

Passu was such a fantastic setting that, when there, we decided to take an early morning walk into the steep rocky mountains. We really didn't have any of our usual climbing-holiday equipment on this trip, and so had to carefully make our way along the very steep and rugged paths wearing cycling shoes. These paths must have been goat tracks as we struggled to keep our balance, but the views made it all worthwhile. Passu is one of the most beautiful working villages I have ever seen, and the picture of us in these mountains remains the home screen photo on my phone to this day.

Farmers and families were harvesting the hay and collecting fruit from the trees.

Gathering hay in Passu
Farmers and families were harvesting the hay
and collecting fruit from the trees

Despite this on-foot bonus I was also growing a little concerned, because I knew that we still had about thirty-five miles of steep roads crisscrossing the valley before we could get to our next destination of

Karimabad later that day, and we had already used up quite a lot of energy, not to mention daylight hours, walking in those mountains.

Having reluctantly left Passu mid-morning, the road wound its way around steep gorges, beautiful fresh streams and some very inviting pools of clear water. I was really tempted to stop again for a swim, but knew that if we did so we wouldn't make it to Karimabad before sunset.

There was also an interesting footbridge that crossed the main river in the valley floor; but once again it was quite a trek to get down, plus we'd have to get back up again to continue along our way – and so we had to make do with a picture, and the now-recurring thought of *That's something else we will have to leave for another trip.*

The road began a gentle but consistent decline. It's surprising how good it makes you feel with the air rushing through your hair and clothes. In such instances wearing loose cotton shirts enabled us to be protected from the fierce sun, while at the same time enabling the wind to have a welcome, cooling effect as it dried the sweat from our bodies.

Karimabad was built on an extremely steep hill, with a fort at the very top, and it just so happened that our lodgings were right beside said fort! *Well that's typical,* I thought, *another hard climb up mountain roads at the end of the day.*

While there, and even though we stuck to bottled water, we were struggling quite a lot with upset stomachs. The water in the room was running dark brown, and looked and smelled terrible. We later traced the water pipe and saw that it led from the gutter in the road outside to a tank that then fed our taps. No wonder – it was unfit even for washing clothes in.

The restaurant food also gave us problems, and it took a while before we discovered a fresh water station in the village. The water there was not great either, but appeared to be clean enough to drink; and to be safe we used our USB-powered ultraviolet water steriliser on it.

We planned to stay in Karimabad for four nights: not only for recovery purposes, but to enjoy the spectacular views that looked directly out from our room onto Rakaposhi mountain. Its name meaning 'snow covered' in the local language, and at 7,788 metres high, it is the twelfth-highest mountain in Pakistan and the twenty-seventh in the world. Sunsets and sunrises were just incredible there and it was such an amazing, beautiful experience. In the local culture these mountains play such an important part in daily life, and you can see why they are treated as being almost godlike.

Karimabad itself, previously known as Baltit, is a great working village with lovely little shops selling handicrafts (you know, the sort of things that you would buy as keepsakes: rock jewellery, carved boxes, paintings), while also figuring as a popular tourist destination. Indeed, the Baltit Fort and Karimabad village had received the World Award of Tourism back in 2000, fighting off competition from locations in Britain, Australia, Indonesia and India. This is well deserved, and came as little surprise to us, as Karimabad proved a truly interesting place to visit. The fort at the top of the hill has a lot of historical interest and was the caravan resting place for people travelling through the Hindu Kush to the Vale of Kashmir. It was also the capital of the Hunza Valley for over seven hundred and fifty years, before becoming part of Pakistan in 1947.

Rakaposhi mountain (7,788 metres) majestically dominates the skyline and is revered in local folklore

While in Pakistan we struggled to get local sim cards for our mobile phones; the government actively controlling their availability. However, we managed to finally obtain one while in Karimabad, thus allowing us to stay in contact with business and family without incurring exorbitant data charges.

Another issue in the country was getting cash, which by now we were running low on. So far we hadn't been able to withdraw money from a single ATM in Pakistan (despite our having eight different types of credit or debit card, and enrolling the assistance of two separate bank managers), and even our dollar supply for exchanging in the local market was seriously dwindling.

One helpful customer offered his support if we transferred money to his account, but this looked a bit too risky – it taking days to clear, and our associated fear we wouldn't hear from him again after wiring him money.

In hindsight, though, his offer was likely a genuinely benevolent and reliable one. During our time in the country, we found the Pakistani people to be extremely generous, always willing to help, and not the type to steal anything. It's just not in their culture. Their lives are very heavily intertwined with their community, and so the status of their family in their village, and their position of respect, is a strong motivator and driver for their actions. Even an accusation of stealing or wrongdoing would have huge consequences for them. We found this to be the case on many occasions, and came to really appreciate their strong honesty and character.

Hearing about our cash-related plight, and as a typical example of the aforementioned trust and generosity, our lodgings host lent us 5,000 rupees to feed ourselves that day. We also met a friendly 'Karakoram Biker' (the Karakoram Bikers being the on-the-ground company who had arranged our visas for us), who gave Pedr a lift on the back of his motorbike to track down a cooperative cash machine in the next village, which eventually worked – thank goodness!

After leaving Karimabad we headed for the city of Gilgit, staying along the way at a small house in a beautiful apple and fig orchard in Nasirabad called Faizan Guest House. Our very friendly host educated us all afternoon about the Hunza Valley people and their near-one-hundred-percent education rate; whereas 'the guys across the river', mostly a different Sunni group, had a much lower literacy rate, especially for women. This education battleground between the sects had proven to be a big issue, with twelve schools having recently being burnt down in Chilas: a village we would cycle close to before branching off up the Babusar Pass.

Descending from Nasirabad

We left Nasirabad early the next morning and after a long, hard and particularly hot cycle ride, took a break sitting on a wall a few miles outside of our destination, Gilgit.

Just then two mature locals walked past us dressed in burqas. We said a friendly 'Hello', but strangely enough they spat across our path. It was the first time we had encountered anything remotely negative and it made us laugh out of pure surprise.

It is very interesting to think back on how different people reacted to us. We were a bit of an oxymoron. On one hand we were clearly British, so they assumed that we must be rich. On the other, we were riding bicycles and often sweaty and dusty. Anybody riding a bike here must be the poorest of the poor – the thought process being that if you had any money at all you would buy a motorbike, and if you were of a reasonable status you would have a car. Status, position and demonstration of wealth were significant factors affecting one's standing in society here; as indeed, unfortunately, they are in many other parts of the world.

The educated there generally thought that we should be treated as rich visitors on a tour of their country, and they couldn't do enough to help us. The less educated, by contrast, just looked at the bicycles and treated us as not fit to be talked to. They may have also assumed that we had different religious or social values and beliefs.

Having arrived in Gilgit, we struggled to find what was the only accommodation venue we had booked while back in England. It was supposed to be a really nice, well-furnished house on the main Sakwar road, which was – of course – near the top of a steep hill.

Eventually, with some local support, we found the place. There was no internet connection, the bathroom had recently collapsed, the sink didn't work, and the shower at best dribbled water: so it proved to be a bit of a disappointment, and certainly not as advertised. They did, at least, have a fridge that had cold drinking water inside, and so we managed to have a makeshift shower using that and a bucket.

One of the locals, who let us into the guest house, was keen to ensure we felt welcome here, and offered to make us milk tea. I assume this was his first ever attempt at making it, though, because he poured milk into the kettle and subsequently seemed surprised that it coagulated around the element! Eventually we convinced him that we really just wanted to drink cold water.

Tabish and Ali of the Karakoram Bikers arrived shortly afterwards and were very helpful and knowledgeable, which was exactly what we needed. They suggested that we hire some motorbikes for a few days to explore a road towards the Afghanistan border. This excursion was not on our planned cycle route, but offered an interesting way to quickly explore more of Pakistan; and – as if we needed it! – was another adventure. Their working process was easy: 'Help yourself;

there are the bikes, pick the best ones'. The cost was £12 per bike per day, cash, to be paid upon their return. No paperwork and no deposit: just trust-based ('Please bring them back').

There were six bikes to choose from. Some had seats that just fell off, others simply sounded as if they were about to explode. One seemed to work properly; while the second motorbike we selected, being the best of the remaining bunch, nevertheless had only a rear brake.

It would be the first time that Pedr had ever ridden a motorbike, and he found the totality of his preparatory riding lesson to be, well, 'Just get on and ride'! In my case it proved to be almost as challenging for me, re-learning to ride, as it was for him as a rookie. I had last been on a motorbike thirty-five years before. Pedr had never seen me ride one.

Riding my bike was particularly complicated by the fact that the front brake didn't work. Worse than that, it actually locked the front wheel if you accidentally pulled it.

Ali was recommending a trip along the 'Gilgit to Chitral' road alongside the Gilgit River to a place named Hāim. It was a long day's riding in a narrow valley on a road that was part tarmac and part dirt track. At some points we just rode over recent landslides that had crossed the route. Approaching the first of these, I looked back at Pedr with a grin and a signal to power up the rocky 'path', as he was clearly concerned that this was the end of the passable road. He soon had a huge shock when, powering up the rubble on our side, he encountered a bus that had done the same up the other side – narrowly avoiding a collision and doing a great job of staying upright. The adventure had just got a little bit more interesting.

You could tell this area was a bit more tense than Gilgit by the reaction we were getting from the locals. They were still mostly friendly – encouraging smiles, thumbs up, welcoming comments – yet there was some definite tension in the air: one waiter making a point of slamming our drinks down and fixing us with a hard stare.

It was just a small minority who were angry or confrontational, and at that time we really didn't understand why. Either way, for the first time we felt uncomfortable enough to head straight back to Gilgit, rather than staying there for the night.

Ali later admitted that two weeks prior there had been a shootout between the police and the Taliban fighters in the very same village we stopped at for lunch. This had resulted in two police and five Taliban dead. Ah! That explained a lot. The Taliban were present here; and some of the locals supported the terrorists' actions, and were thus against people like us being in their homeland. We had even encountered a few instances of graffiti on the road exhibiting anti-Israeli and anti-US sentiment.

We asked Ali why he therefore had recommended for us to go there. He just shrugged, and said he thought it would probably be safe now, as they had since increased the numbers of police in the area! Safety is all relative here, clearly: they had bigger things to worry about than motorcycle licenses and legal bikes!

The next day we took the motorbikes back out, this time along the Karakoram Highway to revisit Karimabad. The road was much better and the riding was fun, weaving through the mountain roads in the sunshine. We also knew that the people there would be friendly. It was amazing, we reflected, how far we had managed to cycle that one time before: as it took us over two hours of hard motorbike riding to cover the exact same distance as a morning's ride on a fully loaded bicycle. No wonder I had found it such hard going!

As I rounded a corner on one particularly steep downhill section, the vehicles ahead of me all of a sudden came to a halt due to a police checkpoint. I knew my lone back brake would not let me stop in time, so a scary rear-wheel skid and sideways slide – along the empty oncoming traffic lane, drifting past at least twenty cars in the process – was just enough to bring me to a stop before the checkpoint barrier. It was an incredibly close call.

Pedr had looked on in disbelief, a look of 'What are you doing?!' on this face, before finally realising that his dad hadn't just turned into a crazy biker but was actually trying desperately to stop without hitting anything.

Later on we misjudged the timing of our return to Gilgit, meaning it was dark for some of our way back. Biking in the blackness through Pakistani villages and towns during the Eid break proved particularly terrifying. Sheep, goats, cows, bikes without lights, and people just crossing the road in front of you without looking, caused mayhem; and cars with full-beam headlights careering towards you on the wrong side of the road are twice as terrifying at night. By now I had also discovered that my bike didn't have back lights or indicators either so it was an incredibly bad recipe all round.

Somehow we made it back to Gilgit in one piece, complete with a million stories of ridiculous things happening along the way. (Incidentally, we had also been told to watch out for ladies dressed in traditional burqas. Apparently, they just walk across the road and have the belief that cars will just not hit them – it's really disconcerting and dangerous.)

We handed the motorbikes back to the Karakoram Bikers and continued to cycle out of Gilgit and into the desert. Ahead was a long trip to Raikot Bridge, Fairy Meadows and Nanga Parbat base camp.

We were heading towards the Himalayas.

HUGE MOUNTAINS AND
BEAUTIFUL VILLAGES

After forty-five miles of pretty hot cycling from Gilgit, through arid rocky landscapes, we bumped into the only other cycle tourists we had so far encountered. They, a Czech couple, were true veterans of the touring world, having been on the road on bikes for the past sixteen years. (Hats off to @cyclingnomads.)

Pedr talked warmly about all the cyclists he had met on his travels and all the fun they'd had swapping stories, providing advice, and helping one another along their way. It was lovely to meet some fellow cyclists and exchange stories and experiences, and a shame that we didn't have more time to spend with them.

The couple suggested that we stay at the Greenland Hotel at Fairy Meadows on the way to the Nanga Parbat base camp. They did, though, warn us that the Chilas road and Babusar Pass were quite dangerous and difficult for foreign cyclists, due to the threat of sectarian violence, and that because of this the police had escorted them most of the way from Islamabad to Raikot Bridge. They also put us in touch with a family they had stayed with in Abbottabad.

After going our separate ways from the couple we took a short break at what is known as the 'triple point' in the mountain ranges: this being where the Karakoram mountains, the Hindu Kush and the Himalayas all meet. We had now crossed into the Himalayas.

A few hours of cycling later, we were in need of some well-earned rest. We stopped at Raikot Bridge at a guest house, before the following day hiring a jeep and a professional local driver in order to tackle the second most dangerous road in the world.

Just as we set off the police stopped the jeep and insisted that they provide us with an armed escort, who promptly proceeded to jump into the front seat. It was apparently dangerous for us in the mountains. This road was the only way up to Fairy Meadows, which was in turn the start of the walking path to the north face of Nanga Parbat – one of the most famous mountains in the world.

For two hours the jeep lurched over the steep, rough and exposed rock leading to the start of the walking track. I could fully see why they only let these professional drivers take people up there: it would have been very easy to lose a vehicle off the side of that track.

We took a short video of our ride in this jeep, with loud Pakistani music blaring from its speakers as we careered up this rugged incline. For fun we then posted it online – to predictably squeaky responses from family and friends back home!

Two more hours walking, still with our police escort in tow, got us to Fairy Meadows. This was a beautiful little mountain plateau: with pine trees, meadow grass and the recommended Greenland Hotel nestled into the mountain. 'Hotel' was perhaps overselling it – it was more of a chalet – but nevertheless this was a magical place set in stunning scenery. It was a really unexpected and pleasant surprise to come across this little oasis in the middle of this severe and exposed mountain.

Fairy Meadows

Greenland Hotel

Theirs is a picturesque and self-sufficient little mountain community. To our further surprise, the chalets had both running water and reliable electricity, unlike the many villages and even cities we had stayed at on our route to date. We asked why this was and they pointed to the electricity generator installed on a little river.

'That's where our power and our water comes from,' was the response. 'There are many big powerful rivers in this mountainous Hunza Valley area,' they then added, 'but there are not many electricity generators.'

When we asked why, they told us how the local water contains a lot of coarse-grained grit and sand from the relatively young mountains and fractured rock. This causes excessive wear on turbine blades, rendering generators economically inefficient and thus greatly lessening their prevalence in the area. I was sure there must be a solution in order to make them more viable, but was even more convinced that many other smart people must already be thinking about this!

Our up-until-then staple diet of dahl bhat started to taste even better while we were in the mountains. Every meal we'd had on the road for quite some time now had been dahl, and I had been beginning to get tired of it, but the community's chef Maroof was not only an especially great cook but a lot of fun to boot. Immediately upon our arrival he had invited us into his kitchen to watch our supper being cooked. It was pretty cold outside, despite our jackets, and the kitchen – where the many other helpers also gathered for a chat, a laugh and joke, and to help make the meals – was also the warmest place around.

We loved learning the job titles of all the locals. One was a horse trainer, another a guide. Then there was a donkey manager (donkeys being available to hire if you required help getting there), a kitchen helper, a naan cooker and even a fire lighter – the chalets having a wood-fire heater in every room, each of which required starting and supplying with wood of an evening.

Our policeman escort had returned to Raikot Bridge by now, and as we set off the next day we were accompanied by a full-blown anti-terrorist squad member complete with a Kalashnikov AK-47 assault rifle.

It transpired that eleven mountaineers had been shot at at the base camp in 2013, and the authorities were still not taking any chances. Our anti-terror escort was also a great guide, with many of his family living in the mountain huts. As we passed these homes they would come out to say hello and offer us chai.

We had not asked for or booked any of these police escorts and were not expected to have done. They simply just appeared and helped us as and when they thought we required it. It was much appreciated – if a little disconcerting that we should need them at all!

The following morning we headed off early for base camp; this being the start of the hard ice-climbing and rock-ascent route up Nanga Parbat. It was extremely tough-going: a very rough, gravelly track rising six hundred and fifty metres in vertical elevation. *We really should be wearing boots!* was my prevailing thought as we headed up into the mountains, before our guard suddenly told us to get down behind a rock and to stay there while he checked out a noise in the woods. It turned out to be a fell runner and of no threat, but was nevertheless a reminder of the situation and the focus demanded of our protector.

*Farmer's hut. They were really welcoming and offered
us chai as we walked past*

Nanga Parbat, on the way up from Fairy Meadows

We eventually made it to base camp, where we found a large memorial with lots of names on it – these in recognition of the mountaineers who have lost their lives on Nanga Parbat. Its north face, Rakhiot, is the largest single ice wall in the world and the hardest route up the mountain. I have scaled quite a lot of mountains, but to me this looked more or less impossible to climb. Reinhold Messner – one of the most famous climbers in history, and whose own brother perished while descending the mountain back in 1970 – still comes here for holidays.

In total we spent eight hours walking that day, and so really appreciated it when we got back down and met the jeep at the top of the track to take us back to Raikot Bridge.

Having returned safely, we started to plan the following few days' cycle route. This stage was going to be difficult. It was steep, long, and over some of the most dangerous sections we were slated to encounter. The route took us close to Chilas and over the 4,173-metre-high Babusar Pass to Naran. It was more than 3,000 metres of climbing and a distance of over one hundred and twenty miles, and so pretty impossible to do in a day. It was also too dangerous to camp on the route, and so we were banking on some police assistance along the way (we thought that they wouldn't let us cycle the Babusar Pass section, and so would hopefully give us a lift!). At least that's what had been provided to the Czech cyclists we had met.

THANK YOU PAKISTAN POLICE

We set off at first light along mixed paved-and-dirt roads. We were determined to make good progress, so kept up a good speed despite the road being much rougher than usual, and really hard going.

The sun resumed its baking-hot intensity and the dusty roads just seemed to make it worse, even at eight a.m. We almost made it to Chilas before we were picked up by the police – 'for our safety' – and taken the next two miles to the Babusar Pass checkpoint. The police asked where we had come from, and were surprised and pleased we had made it this far intact.

After registering at the checkpoint, the police promised us a lift to the top of the pass. They point-blank refused to let us cycle it.

Time passed as we patiently waited by the side of the road, accompanied by a policeman. However, when the lift we had been promised didn't materialise, we started getting concerned that we wouldn't have enough daylight hours left to cycle to Naran. And so we started hitching a lift. When one truck did kindly stop, all of a sudden our armed policeman jumped in its front seat, secured our bikes flat in the back, and proceeded to instruct us to stay out of sight in front of the bikes at the rear.

Babusar truck ride
Heading up the Babusar Pass after hitching
a lift along with our police escort

Ok well, that works, we thought, *but what's all the fuss all about?*

Well, we were about to find out!

Men with big wooden poles with whips attached to their ends were waiting at a broken section of the road, and chased the truck to see if they could get us in the back. Then not long after we saw some kids, armed with slingshots, who fired stones that rained down on us, as well as many other guys who were clearly looking for trouble.

In fact, we came to learn, this road was a known hot spot: one so dangerous that the police close it to all traffic at night.

Lucky we had an armed police escort to look after us!

WINDING ROADS THROUGH MOUNTAINS AND VALLEYS

We registered with the local checkpoint at the top of the Babusar Pass before setting off once more. We had too many miles to negotiate to reach Naran, so we just peddled like mad down the long pass, covering as much of the distance as we could.

We passed through a village with a burned-out tanker on the side of the road and which offered, on first appearances, no particularly comfortable lodgings. There were groups of people in the streets, staring at us as we peddled into their town. With the light fading, no place to camp, and steep rocky hillsides all around, we had no choice but to stop in order to try and find somewhere to sleep.

Within a few minutes of doing so we were discovered by a group of five people dressed in traditional robes and headgear. They walked quickly and purposefully towards us.

I asked Pedr to go into the main village hotel and ask if there was a room available that night. Meanwhile I tried to defuse the situation with the these people now surrounding me.

They asked politely what we were doing here, and what religion we were. I knew that this was a tricky question to answer. We clearly were not Muslim, and saying we were either Christian or atheist both carried their own serious risks.

I said that we had no strong religious allegiance, but were a father and son travelling through their great country to get to know the people and villages along the way. Fortunately, one of the most important things for a father to do here is to take his son travelling. They listened and then left me alone; regrouping to one side, talking intently between themselves.

Then the man dressed in white robes approached me and extended an invite for us to dine with them. This seemed like less of an invitation and more something we shouldn't refuse. We wanted to get changed out of our cycling gear and get washed. They all waited patiently as we did so, before taking us down the street to their mosque.

At the mosque we observed the requisite washing ritual, and were then provided with slippers. Our new friends then gave us tea and biscuits along with the elders, before we sat through their prayers and sermons, which they kindly translated for us.

Then they rolled out a carpet for us all to sit on, and gave us a truly lovely meal – the best we'd had since arriving in Pakistan. The meal, we found out, was the result of their Eid festivities – wherein the richer farmers give one of their animals to help feed the local poor in the community – and we were being treated as the ones receiving the food, as guests of the village. This hospitality was much appreciated, and we were very thankful.

I was paying very careful attention to the preachers, listening intently and replying in the best way I could to ensure we properly communicated that we appreciated their generosity and learnings.

Just as the prayers and sermons were about to start a man came into the mosque carrying a Kalashnikov AK-47 assault rifle. We knew it was an offense to carry this weapon unless you were in the police or army, but felt very vulnerable (as well as surprised to see this in the mosque).

We thought for a while that we had been set up, but there was not much we could do at this stage other than to watch and listen intently, albeit with some apprehension. We were polite all the while and looked for a way to escape, but at the same time it was very interesting hearing what they had to say, and understanding their beliefs and preaching.

I was perhaps a little too convincing, because Pedr later asked if I had suddenly been converted, and said that the person he talked to had suggested that he should listen to his dad!

I guess it's surprising how convincing you can be when you are in a strange town, in a dangerous area, with groups of religious people in a mosque, one of whom is carrying an AK-47 rifle!

It turned out that the group of five people that had surrounded us as we entered the village were actually local mosque elders and Islamic preachers just having returned from Somalia. They were actually protecting and looking after us in their village.

In the aftermath, we were informed that there are no absolute rules in Pakistan, provided you have money, and provided you don't then get caught. Granted, these people were talking about the rules of the road – but it appeared to apply to everything.

As for the roads, it was absolute *chaos* on them, with the rule of 'critical mass' seeming to be the only one worth sticking to. In other words: *If there are enough of you, then all go together, and the other guys will stop.*

We were escorted back to our accommodation by the white-robed preacher. Once there, he informed us that their cook would stay up through the night at the base of the stairs to protect us. We had been mobbed with selfie requests and lots of questions, with a group of young locals keen to talk to us way into the night. However, we really needed our sleep.

Before he departed, the preacher asked if we would go with them to visit a local school the next day and meet the children. We were really torn. This would have been great to do, but we knew we needed to cycle early in the morning to avoid the heat of the day and to cover, on the rough and challenging roads, the miles to the next available place to stay.

And so we politely declined, but I would really have liked to have accepted. You don't get many invitations to do that sort of thing, in that sort of area, and it would have meant a lot – both for these people and for us.

We also remembered the main piece of advice the police had given us, which was to keep moving and not linger in any one place. This, they said, would help us avoid potential trouble. So we prepared to set off early the next day.

Before sunrise we started cooking our morning porridge in the bathroom (the explanation for this location being that it was the largest space we had access to, plus we were mindful not to disturb anybody so early on). We had a long way to go that day and were very much still in the steep mountain areas, where it was surprisingly cold. The road itself was very up and down, with many non-tarmac areas, loose stones and huge potholes, and with rivers crossing it. The largest potholes always seemed to come just before the next big uphill section. Albeit against a picturesque setting, it would prove really hard work: a never-ending cycle of switchback roads alongside some beautiful valleys, villages, lakes and rivers.

Pedr's Bike by Lulusar lake

Mountains descending to Naran
The mountains here are remote but fertile, with farming being the
main business. The roads are steep and undulating as they wind
through the valley and across streams

Indeed, it was so rough I managed to break three wheel spokes, needing to stop by the roadside to replace them. The broken spokes were on my rear wheel on the cassette side: which meant removing the wheel, the tyre, the inner tube and the cassette, before rethreading the spokes and then tightening it all up (not easy!).

Replacing the broken spokes

In hindsight, we were fortunate to have so few breakages. Both bikes had strong steel frames and the wheels boasted the full quote of spokes. This would be the only time we had to replace any of them.

After the repair we just kept cycling, hour after hour, until the light started fading on us and we again crawled into another little village. This one had a reasonable hotel, The Glorious Continental Hotel, which boasted, on a big billboard outside, that it came with Wi-Fi!

This would be the first internet connection we'd had in about a week, so we booked in. As were we gulping down a large, cold (and very welcome) drink, the local politician and his support team turned up. They wanted their picture taken with these strange British men in their village: a marker of how rare it is for them to see cyclists here.

This area was still viewed as being too dangerous for us. The hotel manager was joined by a local politician and, without telling us, they had organised an armed guard (with yet another AK-47) to stand outside our room all night. It was a really weird experience; and quite strange, considering we hadn't really felt in any way threatened. We were clearly just not aware of all the dangers.

Regardless of the fact that they were clearly motivated to not have foreign travellers executed in their town, it was nevertheless so good of them to look after us like that.

Once again, as soon as there was enough light we set off – on the final stretch of the road to Abbottabad. We wanted to arrive in reasonable time, in order to meet a family who had offered to put us up. This family had been recommended to us by the Czech cyclists we had passed in Gilgit.

WELCOME TO ABBOTTABAD

Cycling into Abbottabad, the traffic was moving quite slowly, even for our bikes. And we soon came up behind a small, open-backed bus. There were two women dressed in traditional burqas sitting in the back of the bus, looking back out towards us. We followed this bus for a while – slowly, and without any interaction – yet before long, being the open and welcoming sort of guy that I am, I really couldn't help myself. I gave them a little half-hidden and playful wave hello. They were certainly amused by this, and by us, as I could see them laughing to each other behind their burqas, clearly enjoying this mischievous interaction. We probably got away with it because we were obviously tourists who didn't know any better.

The Pakistani people are very proud of their nuclear missile capabilities. Though we were still somewhat surprised, a little further down the road, to find a roundabout that had a big missile in its middle. Further afield, too, we also encountered a number of other roundabouts displaying all sorts of different broken Indian military hardware (one boasting a helicopter, another a tank) – our assumption being that these items were captured from the Indians some time ago as spoils of conflict.

It was quite strange for us to see these artefacts displayed, showing off their country's nuclear capabilities and war gains.

Missile on a roundabout approaching Abbottabad

In addition to this, we were very aware of the deep-seated historical and religious tension between India and Pakistan: this long preceding, even, the establishment of the republics of India and Pakistan in 1947/8.

One local jokingly told us that the British had abandoned Pakistan in 1947, and, if they had stayed, it would have been much better off! Well: that was way before my time, plus I really do think his aside was a humorous conversation-starter rather than a serious sentiment. As I believe at the time their country was glad to see the back of British rule – and with good reason.

Abbottabad was seriously overcrowded. The rubbish collections couldn't keep pace with the waste generated, and as a result garbage was piled up all over the roads This was such a huge contrast to the Hunza Valley and the beautiful mountains we had cycled through.

Our Czech-matchmade host Mohammad welcomed us to his home with clear excitement over the fact that two hot and bothered foreign cyclists had asked to stay with him for a few days. And what a great stroke of fortune it was that we had been put in touch with this family. Mohammad's mother, father and sister all gave us a really warm welcome (as well as an always-much-appreciated cold drink) in their beautiful, pristine lounge. Though I did feel quite embarrassed: what with Pedr and I both being very dirty and smelly, having cycled all day through the scorching heat.

It was great to be able to talk openly with such intelligent and interesting people in Abbottabad; a place so strange and interesting for us. We were very aware of the different lifestyles, beliefs and government control systems that operated in Kyrgyzstan, China and Pakistan. And so it always made sense to be careful about what we said and how we responded to situations, as we really didn't want to upset or anger anybody. After all, we were here to learn: not to preach or push our beliefs, views or thoughts. That said, this family were really so very kind, and were proactively happy to talk to us about all the things they thought could cause us problems, and which we therefore really ought to avoid.

On a separate note, Mohammad's father shared a lovely story with us about when he was growing up in Abbottabad. He said everybody used to help themselves to fruit from the many such trees that existed in the neighbourhood. He remembers laughing when he first saw somebody in the local market with a fruit stall.

Ah, he thought, *that guy's never going to sell anything!* But that was a long while back, and things have since changed. There is now a strong market culture for food, vegetables and fruit here, just as there is everywhere else in the world.

He also talked to us about how Abbottabad got its name. An Englishman named Major James Abbott had spent eight years establishing the community, which was considered as 'a place of living', and wrote a poem in its honour. So much did he do to establish the city, and so well respected was he as a gentleman, that the locals named it after him.

Although James Abbott's beautiful poem talks about the sweet Abbottabad air, it hadn't been quite so sweet when we cycled into town. And we soon learned how, in the past few years, there has been such a massive influx of people relocating to Abbottabad that it has overwhelmed the city's community resources almost to breaking point. This is partly owing to recent troubles in neighbouring Afghanistan, as well as Abbottabad's great position above the hot low plains of southern Pakistan and close to the mountain ranges making it an ideal place to stay.

There is also a very active military training centre there, plus lots of great medical facilities, as well as a thriving city community.

It is such a shame that it is so overrun with people. Indeed, I was a little sad not to see the many fruit trees that Mohammad's father talked about, and assumed that the land had instead been cleared to make way for more buildings over the years.

Mohammad's sister was a very bright, educated, confident, sociable and beautiful woman likely in her early thirties (we didn't directly ask her age, but she had completed a lengthy education and had a good career). It was a pleasure to spend time talking to her in their house. She was a medical doctor practicing in Abbottabad and was soon to get married. We were invited to her wedding that October, and would really have loved to be there. However, we were short of time and really could not wait – nor easily return! – so reluctantly we had to decline.

The whole family, as you would expect, were excitedly preparing for this landmark event. It was to be an arranged marriage; her mother and father having used their contacts and their best judgement to select the most appropriate husband for their daughter.

This came as a big surprise to us. Their daughter was clearly very smart, and was educated, socially interesting and beautiful. In our eyes she would have been quite capable of meeting and making a good choice of her own partner in life. That said, we talked to her at length about this decision and she was genuinely really happy about the arrangement.

In this community, the relationships, respect and extended family bonds are hugely important and deep-seated. Each family works hard to establish and maintain these relationships, and the ties forged as a result are very strong. Even the hint of wrongdoing is taken very seriously. It is, fundamentally, why theft is rare and families and communities so close-knit.

Maintaining this family unit as your children grow up and establish their own families is equally important. And when marriage follows a successful education and career it is important to uphold community cohesion, and therefore arranged marriages are common.

It was nevertheless still quite a surprise for both me and Pedr. We would never have considered this approach in our family. As parents, me and my wife would of course freely provide our thoughts and as much guidance as possible to our sons and daughters. (We would do this whenever asked. Or when we thought best. Or, most likely, when we simply couldn't stop ourselves!) Though ultimately we took the view that it had *nothing to do with us*: the rationale being that our children needed to live with the consequences of their decisions, and so it was best they made their own life choices.

We were even more surprised to find that, when Mohammad's sister, got married, she would have to stop practicing as a doctor. This came as quite a shock, and also seemed so unnecessary – their being as short of good doctors here as everywhere else. Once again, though, we talked this through, and their perspective was that, to start a family and spend time with them, a busy career would prove difficult to maintain. *Yes, I do know about that one!* I thought. My wife has always worked, and to this day still enjoys her work immensely.

However, they continued, if she continued to work it would have a big effect on how her husband would be viewed in their new social group. And her continuing to be a practicing doctor would likely affect their social balance to such a negative extent that she now felt she would be happy to instead refocus her time and energy to bringing up her children. This was contrary to everything that we felt and did in our family and in our own lives, but I truly felt that Mohammad's sister was entering into this arrangement in order to start her family, and that this was the most important deciding factor. If that meant changes to her work life, then she was well aware of that. She may have already delayed starting a family because of it. We didn't discuss that question with her: it seemed too personal. Anyway, it was a positive choice. The alternative would likely require her to move and to start a new life in a different town, city or country, and that really was not what she wanted. Being near her family was really a key part of this.

Hers was such a brave decision; plus it made me think twice before shouting about my beliefs and values as the only ones that count.

Another stark cultural contrast is that it is generally much more difficult for young women in this part of Pakistan to interact socially with men of a similar age. Even cousins and family members stick to fairly strict social norms governing all interactions. One group of boys told us they couldn't sit on the same bench as their female cousins, or be seen talking to them individually. It would not be okay for them to approach the girls' bench; though, on the other hand, it would probably be tolerated if we were to sit on the same bench as them, as we were foreigners and didn't understand these unwritten rules.

In this community, as everywhere else in the world, there are many 'normal/naughty' interactions that take place and are whispered about among friends. This probably makes it even more difficult for teenagers to understand what is a 'normal interaction' between peers. It certainly enhances the mystery and tension between the sexes at an early age, and to my eye that doesn't appear to be very healthy. Hey, but that's just our perspective, and we really have no idea of the extent of this, or the challenges it creates. We merely had a similar type of story related to us by many different groups of people: one of which was a friend of Mohammad's that studied at a local college, whom Mohammad introduced us to. This friend told us that he had met a girl that he thought could be his wife. Though when I say 'met' her, it turned out that they had just shared admiring looks, and that he hadn't actually spoken to her yet, though he planned to do so.

She was from Afghanistan, and her family lived in a village there. He told us that this was causing some heated discussion between him and his family. It could significantly affect the family's standing in their community, he explained, and this may make it difficult to live normally, and without being degraded in his social groups. We were surprised by the extent of this potential knock-on, but at the same time knew we had too little understanding to provide any useful comment or support. Yet I did write him a message after we left, saying that his family were very wise in being aware of this predicament and he should at least listen to their input. He was gracious in his response to me. 'Thank you Peter,' it read, 'I was so happy for your message, it shows you think about me as your son. I hope you guys come back here soon.'

Abbottabad has recently become infamous for being Osama bin Laden's home and operational centre. That is a bit of a shame, because it misses so much of the positive nature of the city and its people.

Interestingly, and maybe a little concerning, was that this operational centre was only a few streets away from Mohammad's house. Mohammad took us to see it, but we were chased away by a guy with a very big, barking dog, who was clearly not happy that we were there, despite the area now being just a broken walled area of scrub, having being flattened after the raid.

Mohammad's father was very well connected in Abbottabad. He had arranged media interviews for us the next day at his office, and later turned out also to be the senior executive of several hospitals and training centres in the area (the latter proving very useful for sorting out a tummy issue that had been plaguing both of us for some time).

The journalists he put us in touch with provided some very good insights. Interestingly, they informed us that Abbottabad was actually pretty safe for us – 'because it's where most of the militants' families live'. We really hadn't had any bad experiences in Abbottabad, and asked the journalists if there were many militant residents who might dislike us being here. 'Oh yes,' they said, 'there are lots of them. You can easily identify them because they won't look you in the eye. Just look around and you will see how they deliberately divert their attention away from you.'

That was new information for us, and a useful added perspective. Apparently they don't want to make eye contact with you for fear of letting you into their consciousness, which is deemed a form of showing weakness.

They also had some more pressing practical advice for us. 'Please do not put anything about your cycle travels in Pakistan on publicly available internet until you leave the country.' Getting any kind of raised profile, while here, was apparently really not a good idea, and for this reason they promised that our interviews with them would not go public until late September.

We thought back on our interview with the Pakistani TV company on the first day over the border from China. And how, in hindsight, maybe that hadn't been such a good idea. However, we found out later that they too deliberately delayed their broadcast, for the very same reason.

Meanwhile, the people we spoke to really loved hearing our thoughts, experiences and our perceptions of their country – and were delighted to learn how generally positive these had been. They clearly love their country, and feel that it has lots to offer both tourists and businesses. Yet are also acutely aware of the largely negative international press.

They were especially pleased to hear of the welcoming and kind nature of our everyday interactions with people along our way. We had been almost universally positively welcomed, with many people giving us food and drinks, and several offering to let us stay in their house.

It's reassuring to know that almost everybody we met was really keen for us to have a good experience in their country, and would do quite a lot to ensure that this was the case.

It was a strange feeling – when sat on the roof of Mohammed's house, in our little rooftop bedroom – hearing quite a lot of automatic gunfire. We were later told that these were probably just celebratory shots, for a wedding or a birthday, and that it was not unusual to hear automatic gunfire. Apparently we were not to worry.

The best time to cycle for us was in the very early morning. On the day of our departure the whole family woke early with us. They packed us a lovely lunch and provided a good supply of drinking water and fruit to keep us going. They were genuinely happy to have us stay with them and said we would be welcome back at any time. We extended an invite to all of them to spend time in England with us.

Mohammad is very adventurous, and I am sure will travel the world when he has the chance, so we look forward to welcoming him sometime.

TOUGH RIDE TO ISLAMABAD

Our next challenge was to get from Abbottabad to Islamabad in one day. It was really hot and humid now, with the temperature forecasted to be forty-three degrees. This was not ideal when trying to haul a forty-five-kilo touring bike, plus we also needed to carry a lot more water in order to cover seventy-five miles of uneven back roads. (Motorways were not an option for us!)

We passed many interesting sights as we plugged away at about twelve miles an hour. Though after about fifteen miles the temperature really started getting to us – this also coinciding with our cycling through an area of horrible, smoky, smelly brickworks.

The dust from these gave us a dark, brick-coloured sheen all over our sweaty, sticky bodies, and was doing a really great job of sapping both our energy and any positive thoughts we had left!

When I finally gave in and asked to stop for a while, we sat in a hedge trying to get a little shade and to rehydrate ourselves using the hot water remaining in my bottle. We shared a look that said, 'What a terrible place to cycle'. I just sat there – completely worn out, hot and bothered, trying to summon some energy – when a particularly strong-smelling and smoky bus, that sounding like it was about to croak, slowly chugged up the hill past us. As it got near the top it ground to a halt, the engine then proceeding to backfire with a big bang, covering us with a nice layer of soot in the process.

The driver immediately jumped out of the bus, ran over to us and asked, in universal sign language, if we could help bump start his bus!

I didn't have the heart to tell him that I didn't have the energy to bump start my bicycle, never mind his bus, but he was insistent: pulling us up and gesturing that we push the bus backwards and that he would bump start it in reverse. I really couldn't see how this was going to work, or how he then expected to get back up that hill.

Nevertheless, we did as requested; and, magically, the bus engine started and it set off back up the hill with renewed momentum.

Well, we just started laughing. What else could possibly happen next?!

As if right on cue, a man appeared with a wheelbarrow and a scythe; singing away to himself while cutting plants from the hedge and collecting them in his wheelbarrow. What on earth could he be happy enough about to be singing in this scorching heat and thick, red, smoky atmosphere?! As he went past he gave us a big smile and a friendly wave, and even posed for a picture!

Puzzled, we checked out his wheelbarrow – and it was packed with cannabis plants! They grow wild out here and are free for all. It reminded me of the Monty Python song 'Always Look on the Bright Side of Life'. Every day there was bringing so many adventures and interesting experiences.

That same night, I was about to collapse from exhaustion in a cheap but friendly Islamabad hotel when Pedr called a guy he had randomly met in Uzbekistan. That man turned out to be the Vice President of the National Bank of Pakistan, and was based in a highly secure area of Islamabad. He instantly agreed to pick us up, right there and then, and take us for drinks amid the beautiful Margalla Hills (snake hills) range surrounding the city, along with his friend, who it turned out worked for Microsoft as an enterprise architect. And so it seemed my rest would have to wait!

I had worked for many years at Sun Microsystems, setting up Java Centres to drive enterprise architecture developments, in the late 1990s, and so we had a bizarre conversation and an interesting evening, sipping fruit juices and discussing corporate finance and enterprise technology. Our two benevolent hosts took us through the secure areas of Islamabad, where you need a special security pass to get into, before dropping us back at our hotel. One of the great things about travelling is that you get to meet all sorts of interesting people you would never come across in normal life.

Shakarparian Tilla Charouni, the highest peak in the Margalla 'Hills', is 1,604 metres high – that's 259 metres higher than Ben Nevis, the British Isles' highest *mountain* – and is a great place to sip fruit juice and look out over the flat city of Islamabad. Four weeks had passed in Pakistan and we hadn't even had a single beer. We understood that alcohol was forbidden; although we were once offered some dodgy-sounding, back-garage 'Hunza water', which we had decided not to try. (The 'drinking water' itself had made us sick, and so risking this Hunza variant seemed like a very bad idea!)

Some time ago the *Telegraph* reported that the Murree Brewery, only eighteen kilometres from Islamabad, made 'world class lager'. The brewery was established in 1860, primarily to meet the demand for beer among the British military and civilian personnel who were posted there. It remains a thriving business to this day. It would have been great to visit this brewery and hear more about its history.

We checked into a small hotel and much to our surprise, it had a little 'Merry Christmas' sign in a basket of flowers in the reception area. It was the last thing we expected to see in August, in Islamabad.

As we cycled through Islamabad a local stopped to talk to us and asked what religion we were. We were naturally reluctant to discuss religion openly, but he volunteered that he was of Christian faith and was keen to extend some friendship. Very nice of him.

We were aware that time was running out, and it was still a long way to Lahore: so, although there was so much more to see in Islamabad, we were motivated to continue our cycle.

LAHORE MARKETS AND MOSQUES

It was getting hotter all the time as we cycled south to lower altitudes, with Lahore on average four degrees warmer (and even more humid) than Islamabad.

Our British bodies were not coping well with cycling hard and long in this heat, and we therefore agreed it was necessary to stay in hotels with air conditioning – as it was simply not possible to sleep in a tent in such conditions.

That said, this was not easy to do: because not many hotels existed between the cities; and, with two hundred miles to cover from Islamabad to Lahore, we were not going to make it in a single day, or in two days even.

We stopped at a cafe along the way and had some much welcomed food and drink. One of the locals insisted that I had one of his 'freshly squeezed' orange juices. The oranges had been baking in the sun all day; the juice squeezer was a very dirty, manually operated machine; and, to top it off, he added a tablespoonful of dirty salt to the drink. Not wanting to upset him, or his group of friends now gathering, I felt obliged to drink it. This was a big mistake, and gave me a very upset digestive system for days.

We continued on our way and as we labored up a particularly long uphill section a car stopped to say hello and offered to put us up in his family's house that evening. We gratefully accepted and cycled into Jhelum where we were introduced to his family.

They were so kind and asked whether they could buy us a present. They were clearly offended when we said that we really didn't need anything, and that they were being kind enough in putting us up. In spite of our renewed insistence, though, we kept being pressed to name anything that we wanted . . .and were eventually asked for our shoe size.

Our host then returned not long after with a pair of new, silvery, sparkly slippers. This was just so strange to us: I don't even own or wear a pair of slippers at home, let alone on a cross-continental bike trip! Anyhow, they were glad to have given us a present. Our host said that showing kindness and hospitality to people travelling through their city was a key pillar of their beliefs, as well as being the right thing to do. It would also bring them luck, he said.

He had a big exam in the coming days, and when we said we thought he would do well in it he was most grateful. We were more than happy to do anything that was viewed as positive, and/or conducive of good luck, as a means of repaying their kindness. Though we would later pass the slippers on to an in-need (and most grateful) man near Lahore. We just hadn't had the room in our panniers for slippers!

Not wanting to impose any more on our kind host and his family, we subsequently checked into the (perhaps inaccurately tranquil-sounding) Tulip Riverside Hotel, which was nevertheless the best that Jhelum had to offer. One night just wasn't enough time for me to fully recover, and so the cycling from thereon would become a huge challenge for me, regardless of whether we set off at the cooler first light the following day.

Interestingly, I found that when I was completely exhausted and had absolutely no more energy to continue cycling, if I then drank half a litre of full-sugar Coca-Cola then it would give me enough power for another ten miles. That was a particularly great discovery, because you could get Coke almost everywhere!

The roadside stench from trash, rotting rubbish and dead animals was overpowering at times, especially as we approached the cities. There were also a lot of flies drawn to this smell, and they hovered all along the hot, dry and dusty roads.

The traffic was manic and just didn't give any room for cyclists, keeping us on our toes the whole time. Cars would drive the wrong way down a dual carriageway because they wanted to turn right, and there was no right turn off the other carriageway – causing swerving-traffic chaos and even greater mayhem for us. Even bus drivers would pull halfway past our bikes and then swerve back in towards the kerb, forcing us to slam on our brakes for fear of crashing into the people at the bus stop.

Most scarily of all, Pedr was very nearly completely taken out when a car hit a motorbike behind him and then they both resultantly struck a concrete barrier. The car brushed Pedr's pannier as it did so, but – very luckily – he managed to remain upright.

Stopping for a Coca-Cola at a roadside tavern, we met a group of men socialising on the table next to ours. One of them had a small bird as a pet, which he pulled out of his pocket to show us. The bird looked happy enough and chirped away as he fed it some crumbs.

As we were leaving, another man – who was on crutches and missing a leg – hobbled near our table, but not so close as to interact with us. After a while the man with the bird walked over to the shuffling man and gave him a coin. We had missed our cue, and so made up for it straight away by giving him some money. We were more used to people being very obvious when they wanted money.

Talking about this later on, we realised that there were many disabled people there, often due to their having been in the armed forces. Such individuals, now unable to do their job, are destitute, and rely on generosity from the locals. Their pride prevents them from being open about requesting money, but now at least we better understood their difficult situation.

Despite the sugar from the drink, I just didn't have the reserves to cover the full seventy-five or so miles we needed that day to get to Lahore (I needed a fully working digestive engine to power my bike that far!); and so, after thirty-odd miles, I caught a lift in a truck for a few miles to take me to the edge of Lahore.

Arriving at our hotel in Lahore, it was still hot and dry, so I quickly jumped in the shower before going back down to the reception. I had a big shock in store when I returned to the lobby. My shower had only taken fifteen minutes, yet in that time the hot, dry, dusty road outside had turned into an intense torrent of dirty water! There was a huge storm raging, and locals were pulling their carts of bananas through storm water right outside the hotel. Just then, a very wet Pedr pulled up outside on a bedraggled bike, though in an equally short space of time the storm abruptly stopped, and everything soon returned to normal.

Lahore water flooding and banana carts
Flash flooding in Lahore

It was great to have made it to Lahore, which meant we were now only twenty miles or so from the Wagah border to India – my destination.

I had pre-booked a tour of Lahore many months earlier – the Pakistani visa application having required us to purchase a tour with a registered travel agent, as well as possessing an official letter of invitation to their country. And so, with humidity hitting eighty-five percent, and in the peak afternoon heat, we suffered a kamikaze-style tuk-tuk ride from our hotel to the walled city. This may have not been what we needed right at that moment, the bike saddle sores being at their trip-long worst, but nevertheless the 'Lahore Walled City and Food Tour' proved very interesting historically, as well as a lot of fun. For the first time we had *somebody else* planning our movements for us on a given day. Their asking us to choose what we wanted to see, and then having them taking us around, was such a novel treat!

The choice and variety of food was excellent. It really was *very* good, and we found that we could eat almost anything without worrying about getting sick – which itself was invaluable, well-timed, and incredibly appreciated.

We went to a mosque inside the walled city and scaled one of its towers. It gave a really beautiful view of the flat, busy and disorganised streets of the ten-million-populated city of Lahore. The history of these ancient buildings is fascinating, their having lived through many turbulent times. It's well worth looking up.

Lahore mosque

WAGAH BORDER REJECTION. THANKS INDIA!

Cycling out of Lahore, we excitedly headed for the Wagah border to cross from Pakistan into India. We would then begin the ascent back from the hot planes of Pakistan to the cool of the Indian Himalayas – *yeee haa!* It was a sweltering thirty-six degrees with eighty-percent humidity on dusty, dirty, stinking roads as we pedaled around the edges of Lahore towards the border area.

After a long time cycling along this straight and featureless road, the dual flags of Pakistan and India were visible on the skyline, marking the border. Getting across required stamping out and invalidating our Pakistani visa, which we duly did, before then crossing the parade gates to the Indian side, where we promptly presented our Indian visa and passports for entry.

A long series of heated discussions followed, and we were informed that, although we had valid visas for India, this particular crossing couldn't process them. This was contrary to what I had been told in London by the Indian embassy, who had even completed the forms on our behalf.

We protested wildly, and tried to find a way for the border guards to get our visas passed to the nearby Amritsar airport, where they could be digitally processed. We even offered to pay for a courier. They started getting really angry and threatened to stop us ever getting into India. We tried all means to sort this out, but to no avail.

We were now stuck in the Wagah border area – not being able get into India, and also not being able to get back into Pakistan because our visas had been invalidated. We started trying to contact the British embassy, in the hope they could help get us out of this impossible situation. Luckily, when we then begged the Pakistani-side's officials for assistance, they were most helpful and agreed to revalidate our visas. (The visas only lasted a further seven days, anyway.) So, very disappointed and very very hot, we began the dry, dusty, dirty twenty-mile ride back to Lahore. By this time we had already changed all our Pakistani rupees into Indian rupees, and so we had no money with which to even to buy a cooling drink of water.

This situation was really not good, and we were incredibly relieved to eventually encounter a Visa-accepting cash machine, which really did save the day.

What an awful, wasted day, we thought, and how completely unreasonable and unhelpful the Indian officials had been. I was really disappointed that, despite our having valid visas, the Indian border guards had been unwavering, and were happy to simply send us back to Pakistan on our bikes in the heat of the day.

Now we had to weigh up whether we were going to try to fly to India; or else get to the Indian embassy in Islamabad, some four hours away by bus, and when there try to get another visa – this time suitable for the manual systems at the Wagah crossing.

Unfortunately, India and Pakistan don't get on, and so there were no direct flights from Lahore to take us the very few miles to Amritsar, India. Instead, we would have fly to Saudi Arabia or a similar third-party country in order to then get a connecting flight to New Delhi. Our bikes would need to be taken apart and packed up in boxes. The flight alone would cost us at least £1,500, and so we opted for the four-hour bus to Islamabad and placed our trust in our powers of persuasion to expedite the visa from the Indian embassy there.

This really wasn't going well. Moreover, Pedr was rapidly running out of time in order to get across the high passes in India, via the Leh–Manali Highway. This highway consisted of several passes over 5,000 metres and was usually snowbound from October, but it is one of the most famous cycling roads in India and so one that Pedr really wanted to cycle.

I was also aware that time was running out for me to get to India on time for my pre-booked flight back home from New Delhi.

ISLAMABAD INDIAN EMBASSY

The hotel in Lahore had agreed to hold onto our bikes while we returned to Islamabad to get the Indian embassy there to swap the electronic visas for paper ones suitable for the Wagah crossing.

The bus to Islamabad went on the motorway, which turned out to be in pleasant contrast to the roads we had been taking on our bikes: its being markedly well maintained, spotlessly clean and akin to many big western main roads.

Upon our arrival in Islamabad we headed straight for the Indian embassy in the secure compound. We were merely asking to swap our valid e-visas for paper visas, because Wagah apparently couldn't process electronic visas.

We filled out many forms, completed the photocopying, presented multiple photographs, paid lots of money, and finally filed it with the embassy . . . who then said it could take weeks.

Well, we didn't even have as much as one week left on our Pakistani visas, and so we ended up having to involve the British embassy, which was conveniently located next door.

We had frantic discussions involving diplomats from the British High Commission (the Vice President no less) and escalated the issue through the diplomatic channels, eventually presenting our case to the Indian embassy – where we were finally promised visas in three working days.

So, stuck in Islamabad for three days, plus the weekend, we decided to see the Pakistan Monument Museum, walk 'trail 3' up the Margalla Hills, as well as taking a ride on some motorbikes (we had left our bicycles in Lahore) to see Murree town and Ayubia National Park.

The Pakistan Monument heritage museum was really interesting. The building itself represents the unity of Pakistan: its seven petals identifying the various different cultures of Punjabi, Baloch, Sindhi, Pakhtun, Azad Kashmir and Gilgit-Baltistan. The museum had many historical interpretations that were different to those we were used to, yet was fascinating nevertheless.

Walking out of our hotel and heading up trail 3, we were looking on the floor around us. This is because, as we walked the six-hundred-and-fifty-metre ascent, we were frequently reminded why the hill's name was snake hill. Not being able to identify a kind snake from a nasty one, we were pretty careful not to disturb any of them. We made pretty fast progress on the steep climb, being quite fit by now, and were rewarded by a lovely lunch, great views and a delicious lime-juice margarita at the top (non-alcoholic, of course).

The views at the top of Margalla Hills, looking away from Islamabad, stretched towards Murree and Ayubia National Park and the mountainous foothills of the Himalayas. It's a vast area of natural beauty, and a very intriguing one too. The views gave us a great incentive to explore this area over the few days we had before continuing our cycling adventure towards India.

MURREE MOUNTAIN RESORT

We hired some motorbikes in Islamabad and took advantage of the time we had to explore the mountain resort and old colonial city of Murree, located in the Himalayan foothills between Islamabad and Abbottabad.

We stumbled upon a hotel/restaurant nestled into a mountain near its top. This had a quintessentially 'British colonial house' feel, and offered a reasonably priced lunch with mango juice set in a non-formal (and very British-looking) terraced garden.

We were later informed that the house had been built for a British couple who lived here prior to 1947. It was really lovely: well-built, and much more solid than the numerous houses and buildings we had seen being constructed while on our present travels.

Murree itself was a lovely mountain resort. The air there was cooler, and I could see why it was one of the most sought-after places in the country to own property.

There were some lovely woodland walks and tracks, too, although we were warned not to venture far. This was because there were also many wild animals there: over two hundred species of birds, thirty-one species of mammals – brown tigers, leopards, flying squirrels – and a dozen or so reptiles – a number of whom a pair of naïve tourists really wouldn't want to bump into by accident.

Murree hotel and restaurant

In addition, there is also the possibility of encountering some wild, upset humans . . . so, all in all, it felt best to avoid taking the wild forest paths alone.

Having waited the agreed three days for our visas, we returned in anticipation to the Indian embassy. However, there was still no sign of them. Further questioning ascertained that the visas had been sent to the wrong place for processing. As a result, we would have to wait two more days.

By this time we had seen almost everything we could in Islamabad, and so we resigned ourselves to waiting in the hotel, reading books, with occasional trips out to the embassy to keep the pressure on. It wasn't really what we wanted to do, but we didn't have much choice.

We visited a bank in Islamabad to get some more Pakistani rupees, and went through a market before heading to a new hotel to check in (the one we were staying in previously having been already fully booked in advance for that particular night). And it was then that we encountered a big problem.

When we reached the new hotel we found that our passports and money had gone missing. We searched back along the route we had taken, and the restaurant we had eaten in, but alas could not find our documents.

Ah, we thought, *this really is not so good.* Not only were we really surprised, and confused as to how we could have managed to lose them, staying in Islamabad without our passports was going to be incredibly difficult. The hotels would not check us in, and they made us contact the Pakistani police and file a report for the missing passports – as this way we would at least be able to book into the hotel.

By now, also, we had met a friendly taxi driver, who had been shuttling us back and forth to the embassy. This man, who was clearly a very wise and trustworthy person, told us that nobody would steal our passports in Islamabad. 'I am sure you dropped them somewhere,' he stressed, and assured us that we would find them again. We were not so confident, and were getting a little desperate by now, but decided not to call home and tell them about the lost passports for fear of creating a panicky reaction. It wouldn't help the situation, and we needed to sort it out here. We retraced our steps again the next morning: first heading to the bank we had been in the previous day, and asking if by any chance they had seen them. The bank teller ushered us into a senior manager's office, and – hey presto! – he presented them back to us, along with quite a lot of cash, in many different currencies, that we had left along with them. Our misplaced property had been found near the ATM we had used, and handed into the bank. We can only guess that we must have left them there by accident when withdrawing cash. It was incredibly unlike us, but nevertheless that was clearly what had happened.

We were asked to write a note to the bank, detailing how we had accidentally lost them yet everything had since been returned properly – because the police would certainly be checking with the bank following our official lost property report. We did just that: documenting how not only did we get everything back, but that the bank had also done everything in their power to inform us that they had found our passports.

Finding them had been unexpected; but, when you consider our previous experiences in Abbottabad – where respect in the community depended on honesty and trust – we were hardly left surprised that it had happened in this manner.

However, with our Pakistani visa only having a few days to run, and our still being without an Indian visa for the Wagah crossing, we still had big roadblocks ahead. But at least we had our passports now.

We checked in with my wife and mother. They were a little squeaky on the call, and getting pretty desperate for us to get out of there! I think the stress was starting to get to them, probably even more than us.

There was a three-day embassy holiday approaching, and only two days left on our Pakistani visas, so in fact we really had no choice but to book the sole flight that was available. It was leaving early the next morning from Lahore, where our bikes were being held for us. It went first to Karachi, Pakistan, then changed to SriLankan Airlines to fly to Colombo, Sri Lanka, and from there on to New Delhi, India. Twenty-four hours of flying, costing £1,500, to just get the across the few hundred metres of road to India. It just seemed crazy.

We were really unhappy with the incompetence of the Indian embassy and their continually broken promises. The Wagah border guards' attitude of intransigence, and their general refusal to help, had just been so avoidable. It really had been a very poor service at every stage. The British embassy, although sympathetic, was apparently unable to help us without raising a 'diplomatic incident', which would have itself been over the top.

STRUGGLE TO NEW DELHI

Now we needed to get from Islamabad back to Lahore, some four hours away by bus. Then we needed to find some boxes to pack the bikes up in Lahore, then pack everything else and somehow get ourselves to the airport in Lahore – all in the next twelve hours. This was going to be tough.

We started off promisingly, narrowly making it to the bus station in Rawalpindi, which was just the other side of Islamabad, and taking the first bus to Lahore. On the journey Pedr started working his magic on social media, asking if anybody knew where in Lahore we may be able to get some bicycle cardboard boxes from, at the last minute and on a Sunday evening no less. After lots of replies and leads and referrals we got really lucky. The owner of a great little bike shop, its name Bikestan Lahore, responded to our pleas for help and offered to reopen his shop at nine p.m. that Sunday and give us some boxes.

He was also kind enough to drive us, with the aforementioned boxes, back to our hotel, which was completely the other side of the city.

We were so impressed and encouraged by the genuine offers of help by and intrinsic generosity of the Pakistani people. They were all so kind and helpful all the time, and I can't imagine getting the same support in such a difficult situation in other countries, ours included! I don't know where we would have been without that man's help. Well, I do: I really don't think we would have made the flight at all! So hats off to Bikestan Lahore.

In Karachi, after an already challenging enough twenty-four hours, our bike boxes came off the airplane completely torn and ripped. *Great.*

We didn't have much tape, but we did our best; and subsequently SriLankan Airlines were very unhappy to take the bike boxes – their being right on the weight limit *and* in a tatty state – and so it took all our entreaties and charms to finally get them to agree to let us fly. We finally arrived, exhausted, in New Delhi airport at four in the morning.

The Holiday Inn hotel we booked actually turned out to be *inside* the airport terminal. Yet by the time we realised this key fact we were now *outside*, and it was therefore no longer accessible. The various taxi drivers started fighting among themselves in order to obtain us and our bicycle boxes, and we had to be quite forceful to remain in control and get a lift to the other Holiday Inn near the airport.

All in, not a great experience; yet we had made it to a nice hotel and when there managed to enjoy a long day of sleep and good food. The 'all you can eat' buffet was a particular boon, of which we took full advantage. We then spent time ensuring that Pedr's bike possessed all the best components from across our two individual bikes, so that he would be in the strongest position possible to successfully continue and complete his cycle. We then repacked 'my' remaining bike into the best bits of the boxes that were left, and strapped them together with lots of sticky tape kindly provided by the hotel.

On schedule, and just about intact – and with many amazing stories and experiences that we will share and recount for many years to come – we said our goodbyes.

We had successfully navigated and enjoyed some of the most challenging and interesting countries in the world.

And we achieved our initial objective of getting to India in one piece.

I flew back home happy to have had such a great time, and privileged to have had the chance to make this trip work for me and for Pedr.

The visa challenges, although frustrating, at the time had by extension enabled us to see some really interesting areas of Pakistan that we wouldn't have visited otherwise.

The knock-on of the embassy delays also meant, somewhat regrettably, that Pedr could no longer cycle along the Leh to Manali highway in India as initially planned. He had just missed the boat, therefore, and would have to take a more direct route.

Almost as soon as we realised this, though, we discovered that there had been blizzard conditions on this road in the few days previous. And so, on reflection, if we *had* made it across the border as planned it is likely that Pedr would have been caught in that blizzard. We were receiving news that there was a big rescue effort underway to get a number of people out of their cars and lorries on this route, and that many people (in those sheltered, heavy vehicles, let alone on a bicycle) didn't make it – and so we may have in fact got very lucky with the delay.

And so it was home for me; and more adventures for Pedr.

I was sad to leave, but so pleased that we had spent so much time together.

Thanks for a huge adventure, Pedr. And here's to the next trip . . .

As I flew home Pedr continued his trip, which would take him on through the Indian Himalayas and beyond to Nepal, Myanmar, Laos, Vietnam, Thailand, Malaysia and Singapore, and then further around the world thereafter. His trip is detailed in his blog posts at pedrcharlesworth.com.

At the time of writing, he made it all the way across Asia to Singapore; across Australia's Nullarbor Plain, Perth to Sydney; and cycled the length of New Zealand. Next he wanted to see South America and the Andes, so flew to Lima in Peru and cycled through Peru, Ecuador and Colombia; took an 'interesting' fishing boat trip around the Darién Gap, arriving in Panama City, and then continued on his bike through Panama, Costa Rica, Nicaragua, Honduras, El Salvador, Guatemala and into Mexico – just managing to get across these borders as COVID-19 was closing them behind him, before the pandemic eventually forced him to fly home from Mexico City.

He has plans to return and continue his cycle on through Mexico and up America's East Coast to New York, where he will have completed his huge goal of an elongated circumnavigation of the world on his bike.

On his trip through Costa Rica, he heard from Oxford University that a place was available for research into one of the challenges of making nuclear fusion a reality. Nuclear fusion is often referred to as a 'mini sun on earth', helping to solve the earth's energy supply issue without creating damaging long-term radioactive waste or burning more fossil fuels.

Today (November 2023), Pedr has one more year to go until he graduates, hopefully with his Dr of Philosophy, and then he may have time to finish his cycle around the world. It would be really great if I can then find another interesting, small section to cycle with him.

He intends to write a book detailing his travels, thoughts and experiences along the way, judging by his blogs this will be a great read, I will publicise this on my website openmatter.com when it is available.

When I got home I sold my shares in the sustainability company just before the COVID-19 pandemic. I then started building another, bigger sustainability software platform for the wider business community, which included energy purchasing and offsetting as well as measuring and managing energy use (zellar.com).

I have now moved on from Zellar to take on Chair and Non-Executive Director positions in a wide variety of companies where the businesses interest me, operating partly through my company openmatter.com.

This work is part-time, giving me space to have more adventures sailing my boat and cycling my bike. I also find it very satisfying to help people and companies along the way.

I am indebted to my wife for 'encouraging' me to take on this huge challenge; and for my mum, who suffered silently as her son and grandson careered across these challenging areas, albeit openly encouraging us every step of the way.

Biggest thanks of course go to Pedr for putting up with his dad riding ever so slowly and stopping to take a breather or sample the food at every opportunity. Also for being such a great cycling companion, and for enjoying every step of this huge adventure with me.

ABOUT THE AUTHOR

Peter is a friendly, open and trusting people-person. He enjoys meeting and working with many types of people and in all different situations. His family has always been his priority: time with them being the most enjoyable and important aspect of his life. It is typical of him that he took the opportunity to spend two months away from his home and business to spend time and share life experiences with his son, Pedr, on his cycling trip around the world, despite the risks and clear challenges.

Peter is as active in his personal life as he is in business: always challenging himself to make the most out of life, with deep-set fundamental belief in fairness and trust. He is a keen sailor, racing dinghies as a child and later getting his Royal Yachting Association offshore license. He has taken his family on many sailing adventures, and sails his boat whenever he has the time between his business and social commitments. He also trained as a pilot, obtaining his Private Pilot License and enjoying the freedom of the skies.

Peter currently holds positions of Chair, Non-Executive Director and business advisor with many companies in different business operations and sectors after a successful career setting up, growing and exiting businesses across many different sectors including technology, telecoms, digital music and sustainability.

Peter now prefers to split his time between his leisure and work commitments, helping a variety of companies and their management teams grow and achieve their objectives. He has really enjoyed the challenge of writing this book and will take every opportunity to have more adventures in the future. Peter's website http://openmatter. com is kept up to date, so please take a look.

Printed in Great Britain
by Amazon